It's An *Even Better* Deal

Paul T Steele BA, FCIPS

 **Professional**

It's an *Even Better* Deal!

ISBN 13: 978-0-07-12487-8
ISBN 10: 0-07-12487-1

 **Professional**

Published by:
McGraw-Hill Publishing Company
Shoppenhangers Road, Maidenhead, Berkshire, England, SL6 2QL
Telephone: 44 (0) 1628 502500
Fax: 44 (0) 1628 770224
Website: www.mcgraw-hill.co.uk

British Library Cataloguing in Publication Data
A catalogue record of this book is available from the British Library.

McGraw-Hill books are great for training, as gifts, and for
promotions. Please contact our corporate sales executive to discuss special quantity
discounts or customisation to support your initiatives: b2b@mcgraw-hill.com.

Printed in Great Britain by Bell and Bain Ltd, Glasgow.

Mixed Sources
Product group from well-managed
forests and other controlled sources
www.fsc.org Cert no. TT-COC-002769
© 1996 Forest Stewardship Council

The McGraw·Hill Companies

Contents

Contents

Acknowledgement

For over 30 years I have been privileged to work within PMMS Consulting Group. During that time I have been involved with many dedicated professionals who have freely shared their experiences and ideas with me. Their vast knowledge gained from heading large procurement or sales functions in multinational organizations has provided me with endless practical cases and examples. My own experience, leading teams and troubleshooting across the globe on a wide range of negotiations has given me the opportunity to use this knowledge to further develop and understand the fundamental business skill of negotiating.

Belief and passion I have seen in abundance among those I have worked alongside. These traits and a willingness to stand up against ill-conceived business fashions and fads are a mark of a true professional.

To all my colleagues and clients, past and present, my sincere thanks for allowing me to work with you and learn so much. I deeply regret that I cannot acknowledge everyone individually. Many have assisted with the production of this book, reading drafts and adding ideas and comments, but there are two without whose assistance and support the book would not have been published: firstly, Sam Tulip, who has used his background in procurement journalism and his knowledge thereof to endlessly read and suggest amendment; and secondly, Jennifer Alston, who has spent interminable hours dealing with the manuscript and endless drafts thereof. I am sure both will be glad to move to another project but not without a very big thank you from me.

Foreword

Negotiation is an accepted, integral and vital part of the purchasing process. As a result of my years in purchasing, I am convinced that the ability to negotiate effectively is a 'must have' competence for every purchasing professional. It is also a readily transferable skill, able to be employed to equally good effect in numerous areas of one's personal life to 'get that better deal'. Someone once said that every conversation is, in some way, a negotiation. This book offers the reader a master-class in the art and science of negotiation from one of its leading thinkers, innovators and practitioners.

At the outset, however, I have to admit that purchasing was not my first career choice. I am a chemical engineer and worked for 22 years in a large, international, oil company. The head of purchasing of its UK operations was seen to be 'a good career development opportunity, offering commercial exposure and hands-on experience – for a couple of years'. I moved into the job, having had no previous purchasing experience, and found I liked purchasing and purchasing appeared to like me. As a result, I have spent the past 25 years in the purchasing profession in the private, public and consulting sectors and during that time was Head of Purchasing with Esso, British Rail and Whitbread Plc, also serving as President of the Chartered Institute of Purchasing and Supply.

In the light of my own experience, and like the author, I have come to the firm conclusion that negotiation skills need to be taught and learned. Great negotiators are not born, although some of us have more inherent aptitude for 'the art' than others. It has struck me that negotiation is, in many ways, very similar to the sports of golf or skiing. It looks easy when you see a pro performing, but that is as a result of the application of skills that have been taught and assiduously acquired over many years and as a result of never-ending practice. Many of these skills are counter-intuitive, which is why you need to learn them from an expert. The same is true of negotiation.

As an example, being an engineer, when I first moved into purchasing, my intuitive reaction was that the most effective negotiating style was, without a doubt, the use of clear, unassailable logic. Who could possibly not be convinced by such a scientific, clinical approach? Expert guidance and observing negotiating pros perform over the intervening years have caused me both to test and to revise my intuition.

You will, I think, find that this book enables you fully to explore contemporary, leading-edge negotiation theory and practice. This is supported by numerous and fascinating case studies and insights from the author's own extensive experience which help to bring the theory to life. Your own negotiating style and approach is continuously tested by 'what would *you* do, faced with this?' challenges.

If you have previously read *It's a Deal!*, this complete rewrite and update will provide you with new insights, case studies and challenges. If not, *It's An Even Better Deal* provides a comprehensive, in-depth, thought-provoking – and entertaining – journey through best practice negotiation theory and practice. Its practical approach and guidance should enable you to analyse and understand your own negotiation style and improve your negotiating performance.

Roger Keeling BSc, Dip Chem Eng, FCIPS

Introduction

Why another book about negotiation? Who is this for, how can they use it, what will they learn?

Many years ago I wrote a book called *It's A Deal*, which sought to introduce the concepts of professional negotiation to, in particular, commercial buyers. *It's A Deal* sold very well and not just because it was used in many training courses – it filled a need, and now there is a need for a revised and updated version, because although basic human and commercial behaviour does not change very much over time, the environment in which we operate certainly has.

I aimed the original book largely at buyers because salespeople tend to receive training, of varying quality, in negotiation – buyers by and large less so. This new edition certainly is not intended solely for buyers, however. Although it is largely couched in the language of Purchasing, I believe there are many insights and pieces of advice that salespeople and those involved in contract management, outsourcing, etc., could also read to their advantage.

Increasingly in business, people have to be both buyers and sellers. Before a purchasing manager gets to negotiate the big deal, he or she may already have had to negotiate internally – to secure project approval, finance and so on. So the buyer, in that instance is also a seller.

There are also many other business functions that require negotiation skills (not least perhaps in human resources), and while I do not expect this volume to be on every household shelf, all of us at times have to negotiate, seriously and for large stakes, in our private lives: buying or selling our cars, our houses; or negotiating with other bodies from the tax people to our neighbours. How well we 'do' negotiation does not depend on inborn gifts to any great extent – negotiation is a skill that can be learned and practised, if not ever quite perfected.

So while I make no apologies for casting this book largely in the language of commercial buyers and sellers, I hope you find it of much wider application.

A demanding buyer or customer is *the* best change agent, driving suppliers and the supply market in whatever business sector to be more efficient and more responsive to needs. We benefit from this every day: retailers, supermarkets, industrial manufacturers, offer us as far as they can what we want to buy, not what it is convenient for them to sell.

Likewise, a demanding salesperson drives efficiency internally and is encouraged in this by a best business practice culture. They signal back what the market wants, not merely the rate at which the market is prepared to take up the existing product or offer.

This may seem obvious but it is not so long ago (and in some industries and countries is still the case) that the seller or provider was king under the influence of governments or monopolistic corporations, competition was muted, and buyers and consumers had largely to take what they were offered in the way of goods and services.

This shift in power and influence is a product of, and has given rise to, professional negotiation. If one side (usually, though not always, the producer) really has the whip-hand – for example in a planned or wartime/emergency economy – negotiation is largely strictly limited in use. But in anything approaching a free market, any situation where there are realistic options available, negotiation becomes one of the most important business (and personal) skills. And like most skills, it is something that can be learnt, practised and refined.

Negotiation is a fundamental part of the drive for productivity and efficiency within and between businesses. But one business relationship does not fit all needs, and nor does one style of negotiation.

As business cycles move over the years the marketplace may become at times, more or less challenging. Over the past 30 years I have advised many of the world's leading companies and most disappoint in that when times are good they take their foot off the pedal in the drive for efficiency. A few organizations mark themselves apart and ignore the fact that business is easier at a given time: they continue to exploit the easier market, add resource and increase their efficiency drive.

I witnessed a presentation at a conference by the corporate purchasing director of a large mining company. In the presentation reference was made to both sides winning in the negotiation. As this book explains, 'win/perceived win' where both sides in a negotiation come away feeling their major needs are satisfied, is the most desirable outcome and the soundest basis for a good business relationship, but win/perceived win takes hard work and skill to achieve. At the end I challenged the individual about this and they responded 'Well we don't really believe it but it sounds good on a public platform and in any case we have been printing money in the past few years; business is that good.' As I write the introduction to this book this company is being taken over by another, smaller organization because of its inefficiencies. I believe it forgot to continue the drive in the good times as well as the bad and now they are paying the price.

In management science and writings there is often a serious disparity between abstract theory and the human reality of the personal and business situation, and it is the blood of the participants that often fills the gap. This book has its feet firmly on the ground and is full of practical advice that, I cannot overemphasize, actually works. Nothing is easier than to denounce something you have not tried before. Nothing is more difficult than to try something new. Try something from this book and it will work in most cases.

But I owe it to you, the reader, to enter some caveats.

Firstly, you are yourself, your own individual. You have ways of behaviour that you are comfortable with (in negotiation or in any other sphere) and ways that you are not comfortable with. Certainly you should use this book to help you to extend your repertoire, to expand your comfort zone and to be able to act effectively outside that zone if necessary. But that does not require you to be totally untrue to yourself. If you feel the way you are negotiating is, in some fundamental sense, 'wrong', then don't do it. That is not only a moral argument, it is practical: the other party, if he or she is any good, will certainly identify and exploit your discomfort.

Secondly, inevitably parts of this book seem to be couched in the language of warfare. We have objectives, strategies and tactics. The person across the table is an opponent, and so on.

Richer men than me have made fortunes translating military theories, from the Ancient Chinese through to Clausewitz, into business terms, with some validity. We use some of the military terms – opponents, strategies, tactics – but this is negotiation, not war. You are not (normally) trying to beat the other party into submission, let alone destroy them. You are trying to build an alliance of the more or less willing. It may be short term, just the present deal; it may have hopes of becoming a partnership of long standing that will conquer the world. Of course you want the alliance to be as far as possible on your terms, but the people you are negotiating with are potential allies, not present threats. If you must think in military terms, think Eisenhower, not Patton or Montgomery.

This book falls into two parts.

Part 1 is designed as an easily read introduction to negotiation, which will help you to understand the thinking and the process that I believe lies behind almost all successful deals.

Part 2 goes into much more detail on various aspects of the subject. Yes, it does include lists of tactics and ploys, but I would urge you to read the whole volume both to gain an understanding of how these can be used to your advantage (and when they should not be) and, more widely, to understand how your own personality; and the overall objectives of your organization (the corporate personality if you will) govern what is and is not likely to work in a given situation.

The appendices contain more information on some of the more arcane aspects of the subject. Throughout I have given examples which, despite the necessary anonymity of the cases, really are true: I have seen, worked with and advised the companies and individuals that have made these mistakes.

But negotiation is fun, if you can master it; it is rewarding both personally and for your business. It is a set of skills that almost anyone can acquire (few are actually born negotiators) and refine. Studying the skills outlined here will certainly improve your commercial career, and quite probably give you some new insights into your own personality and private life!

So, read, learn (and enjoy!) for to succeed you will need to negotiate. Before beginning the book ask yourself the following:

- Will computers negotiate in my lifetime?

- Will computers ever move someone to do something other than what they wanted?

- Will people stop telling lies in ten years? (not that lying in a negotiation is advisable).

And go on and *Explode Your Thinking!*

- Be demanding: you are the best change agent.

- Lose your temper and you are the victim.

- Beware of non-opportunistic behaviour portrayed precontractually.

- Recognize that opportunistic behaviour goes with modern economic life.

- Power is not a must for skilled negotiators, but rather knowledge of the situation they find themselves in.

- Small buyers – you are more powerful than you think!

Enjoy this complete rewrite of the original *It's A Deal*.

Paul T Steele
PMMS Consulting Group Ltd
Northchapel House
Horsham RH12 1RD, UK
www.pmms-group.com

Royalties from this book will be donated to:
The Handicapped Aid Trust
The Old Bakery
Green Street
Lytham FY8 5LG, UK
Registered Charity Number 284791

Part 1

Setting the Scene

1

Negotiators are made, not born.

A large part of our lives, almost from the day we are born, is spent in negotiation: with parents and siblings to start with; later with teachers, employers, co-workers, bank managers, traffic wardens, tradespeople and our own children (although nothing in this book is warranted to apply to negotiation with teenagers … or is it?). It is easy to assume that everyone can negotiate quite naturally in the same way that 'everyone goes shopping, so anyone can be a commercial buyer'.

Some people appear to be natural negotiators: credited with charm, persuasiveness, winning ways, 'a born salesperson', they win every point; indeed, the deal seems to be half over before they enter the room. Other people, on paper equally knowledgeable and qualified, seem to lack this special something; they appear, particularly to themselves, to be forever on the defensive, always backing down, never quite in control of the way things are going, a liability, easy meat for the born salesperson or natural negotiator.

But with rare exceptions, natural-born talent has very little to do with successful negotiation. The top salespeople, who are winning negotiators, the dominant diplomats and politicians, are trained, and continue to train themselves, to succeed. They see negotiation as a process which can be analysed, practised, rehearsed and refined; they prepare beforehand and debrief themselves afterwards; they note what tactics and approaches work for them in particular circumstances, and with specific opponents. They understand the rules and can rapidly tell whether the other party knows the process or not.

In other words, successful negotiation is based on a set of knowledge and skills, applied to a problem, which anyone can learn. Effective negotiators are made, not born, and as with any set of personal skills, learning lasts a lifetime. There is a framework, which Part 1 of this book sets out to describe, working within which anyone can rapidly begin to increase their effectiveness as a negotiator. The same framework and skills can be applied, not only in the obvious arena of negotiating with customers and suppliers, but also, with minor variations and rather different constraints, to a range of situations from industrial relations to internal policy and strategy determination (in practice, business professionals may find that negotiations within their organizations are at least as big a part of their lives as negotiations with external bodies).

But what is successful negotiation? In some ways it is easier to say what it is not. Negotiation is not a form of warfare; neither is it about using power to beat the other party into submission, as sometimes practised by large organizations. The Treaty of Versailles in June 1919 (Beckett, 2002), after the First World War, is probably the best example of a 'negotiation' which in fact was nothing of the sort. (Terms were dictated to the Germans with no opportunity for them to make counter-proposals, or to point out that some aspects such as reparations were beyond their abilities. The result was the rise of Hitler and another war.) Negotiation assumes that both sides have some valid starting point, that each has something to offer the other, and that there is at least the possibility that each side can come away from the table with an acceptable deal.

If negotiation is not a war, nor is it a game or a duel. There are many people who derive great enjoyment from the cut and thrust of negotiation, and why not? But there is always the danger that the sheer fun of using some clever tactic, of manoeuvring the opposing party into a corner, tripping them up, catching them out, putting one over on them, can completely obscure the real objective: that of reaching an agreeable conclusion. Tactics and ploys have their place, and we will look at some of them in Chapter 11, but they are only a means to an end.

A negotiation is successful when it achieves its ends, its objectives. Therefore negotiation necessarily starts with an identifiable need and the setting of consequent objectives. Almost always, that will be 'objectives' (plural). Even in the most straightforward negotiation there will be several, perhaps many, objectives, of varying importance and relationship to each other. Often, you can categorize them into need, want and like; for example, 'I need a 5 per cent reduction in unit price' may be the prime objective set by your organization; 'I want daily delivery' may not be absolutely essential, but perhaps of great value to you (and so may or may not be tradable against part of that 5 per cent); 'I would like consolidated monthly billing, and the cartons overprinted with our logo' may be matters not important enough to stall a negotiation, but worth getting if you can. In this example, obviously, coming away with everything except the price reduction hardly counts as success; but equally, achieving that but not even trying for some of the lesser benefits as well cannot be called effective. Your objectives, and their relationships, are key to the whole negotiation process and need to be constantly kept in mind. My research shows that all too often negotiators lose sight of their objectives, so I cannot overemphasize how important it is to keep objectives in mind and clear.

In practice, objective-setting is more complex; on price, for example, you may have a highly optimistic (ideal) figure as your initial position, a minimum (fall-back) figure which if not achieved means a deal is not possible, and between the two your own assessment of the likely achievable outcome – an assessment that you may need to modify as further information is revealed during the negotiation (realistic figure). Fisher and Ury (1981), in their book *Getting to Yes*, looked at this via what they called the best alternative to a negotiated agreement (BATNA): a standard against which any proposed agreement is measured. Not how a proposal stacks against your predetermined bottom line, which may or may not be soundly based, but how the proposal matched your realistic alternatives. The more attractive your alternative to the proposed agreement the more power you have. The fewer your alternatives and the less attractive they are, the less power you have. To develop your BATNA, list all the things you could conceivably do if you fail to reach an acceptable agreement and convert the most promising alternatives into practical options.

Objectives, of course, have to be set in the context of the real world, not just in terms of what may be physically, technically and commercially desirable (and in some negotiations, for example in industrial relations, add 'legally possible'), but in terms of the relative influence and importance of each side to the other. This is not the place for a treatise on key account sales management or strategic procurement, but some readers will be familiar with the concepts of supply positioning and supplier preferencing (Steele and Court, 1996) (see also Chapter 8) and these four box matrices have a critical influence not just on the objectives set, but on the whole planning and conduct of the negotiation.

The supply positioning matrix relates business risk and value of spend (for a particular commodity or for all the supplies from a particular vendor, as appropriate) and suggests a range of behaviours. These range from the low-spend, low-risk situation (where purchasing can be to a significant extent automated and there is really limited use for negotiation) to situations where the priority is to secure supplies, or to maximize profit, or to manage the business relationship perhaps as a longer term partnership. Each will require a different approach to negotiation.

As a buyer, you know, or should know, where a particular deal lies on this matrix. What you do not know for sure is how your supplier sees things. On a similar matrix (supplier preferencing) a supplier may relate the attractiveness of the buyers to the percentage of income it represents. If the supplier sees a buyer as a key account and the buyer envisages the supplier as a potential long-term partner, that is fine; but if the supplier regards the buyer's strategically critical supply as a low-value, low-profit nuisance, a different approach is called for. I will look at this more closely in Chapter 8.

It is worth noting in passing that although this approach is framed in terms of suppliers and buyers, the principle applies to any sort of negotiation. You may find it amusing mentally to relabel the axes to cover an industrial relations situation (where the 'supplier' becomes the workforce or its representatives) or an internal bid for capital expenditure (with the finance director as 'supplier').

But something is missing from the discussion so far, something so obvious that most books on purchasing or sales management completely ignore it. If negotiation were really described by this mechanistic world of 4×4 matrices, surely we could just slot in the numbers and let the computers take over? This does not work: ask anyone who has tried to use procurement software written by non-purchasers. Algorithms do not negotiate (although superficially they may appear to) and despite what it says in the management texts, organizations do not have relationships, people do. Negotiation is a human activity, conducted between individuals (or small teams of individuals) and so is overwhelmingly influenced by human factors: likes and dislikes, fear and threat, voice tone and body language, comfort or discomfort, even the weather.

The 'natural salesperson' or 'born negotiator' does not earn that title through superior knowledge, a better grasp of facts or the ability to perform discounted cash-flow calculations in his or her head (although all these may help). Most are successful in negotiation because they know how to recognize and work with human behaviour, their own and that of the other party.

Born to sell?

A number of years ago in the English county town of Shrewsbury I had an uncle who ran a gentlemen's outfitters. Nobody bought just one of anything from him and they usually left the shop with more than they planned to buy ... AND HAPPY TOO! His shop had a relaxing corner, with fresh coffee and tea with magazines; the whole environment, and people who worked within, oozed warmth. Many clients travelled long distances to buy from him. However, he would be the first to acknowledge that he had been trained, learnt a lot from others about selling and made sure his staff were trained regularly.

I will explore this further in the next chapter, looking at both overall behaviour and the particular styles that people tend to adopt in negotiation. In preparation, here is a questionnaire[1] to help establish your personal negotiation 'style profile'. What it all means will be revealed in the next chapter, but for now remember:

Negotiation is a process in which parties move from their initially divergent positions to a point where agreement may be reached.

Negotiation Style Profiling Questionnaire

How do you see yourself?
  Can you recognize your own approach to negotiation?
  There are 15 pairs of responses to the situation/case study described below. For each pair there are a total of 3 points to be allocated 3:0, 1:2, 1.5:1.5 and so on depending on how you think you are most likely to respond. Do not ponder your answers: it is the gut reaction that is revealing.

Case study scenario

You hire digital relay units and the contract for supply and maintenance is up for renewal. Your supplier, who you have used for a while, supplies decent equipment and service quality is good though not excellent. You have been hiring seven units but now want nine, and therefore are looking for a price reduction in unit price. You would settle for a no price increase; your boss would be satisfied if an increase was held to 5 per cent. Your supplier's first offer, taking into account the increased volume, is at the same unit price as last year. How do you respond?
  Complete the following personal questionnaire to determine your negotiation style.

Instructions

Remember allocate a total of 3 points across each pair of statements below, in the ratio of your personal preference. Single decimal places are acceptable.

---

1 Adapted from Tony Shelley's PMMS/NRI Group Training Booklet.

1	Accept the offer	A	
	Explain that you were looking for a 10% reduction, ask to be met halfway, i.e. 5% reduction in the unit price	C	
2	Explain that you should also be looking elsewhere as a matter of company policy	T	
	Stress the 29% increase in business you have to offer and the fact that the basic cost of the equipment has fallen, due to improvements in technology	L	
3	Suggest improved payment terms and a longer contract period in exchange for a better offer	B	
	Show appreciation for the offer that has been made and mention the 'bad time' users have given you over servicing	E	
4	Accept the offer	A	
	Stress the 29% increase in business you have to offer and the fact that the basic cost of the equipment has fallen due to improvements in technology	L	
5	Explain that you were looking for a 10% reduction, ask to be met halfway, i.e. a 5% reduction in the unit price	C	
	Suggest improved payment terms and a longer contract period in exchange for a better offer	B	
6	Explain that you should also be looking elsewhere as a matter of company policy	T	
	Show appreciation for the offer that has been made and mention the 'bad time' users have given you over servicing	E	
7	Explain that you were looking for a 10% reduction, ask to be met halfway, i.e. a 5% reduction in the unit price	C	
	Stress the 29% increase in business you have to offer and the fact that the basic cost of the equipment has fallen, due to improvements in technology	L	

8	Explain that you should also be looking elsewhere as a matter of company policy	T	
	Accept the offer	A	
9	Suggest improved payment terms and a longer contract period in exchange for a better offer	B	
	Stress the 29% increase in business you have to offer and the fact that the basic cost of the equipment has fallen, due to improvements in technology	L	
10	Explain you were looking for a 10% reduction, ask to be met halfway, i.e. a 5% reduction in the unit price	C	
	Show appreciation for the offer that has been made and mention the 'bad time' users have given you over servicing	E	
11	Suggest improved payment terms and a longer contract period in exchange for a better offer	B	
	Accept the offer	A	
12	Stress the 29% increase in business you have to offer and the fact that the basic cost of the equipment has fallen, due to improvements in technology	L	
	Show appreciation for the offer that has been made and mention the 'bad time' users have given you over servicing	E	
13	Suggest improved payment terms and a longer contract period in exchange for a better offer	B	
	Explain that you should also be looking elsewhere as a matter of company policy	T	
14	Explain that you should also be looking elsewhere as a matter of company policy	T	
	Explain that you were looking for a 10% reduction, ask to be met halfway, i.e. a 5% reduction in the unit price	C	

15	Accept the offer	A	
	Show appreciation for the offer that has been made and mention the 'bad time' users have given you over servicing	E	

Now note your total of points for A, C, B, T, L and E.

Results

	Score
Number of points against A	
Number of points against C	
Number of points against B	
Number of points against T	
Number of points against L	
Number of points against E	
Total	

Your Negotiation Profile
Shade in the squares below according to your score

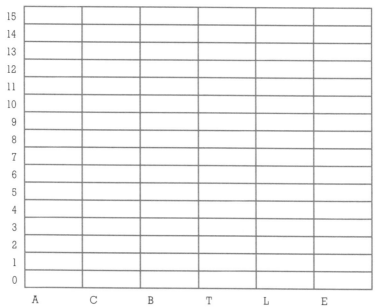

To see how you fared read Chapter 2.

Remember

1. Negotiation skills can be learned.
2. Get training to become effective.
3. Know where your deal lies on supply positioning and supplier preferencing matrices (see Chapter 8).
4. Set different levels of objectives.
5. Remember negotiation is about creating movement.
6. Identify your own preferred style of negotiating.

2

Negotiation Styles

If you are about to negotiate with someone identify their preferred style of negotiating.

Behaviour breeds behaviour. For example, buyers tend to get, if not the salespeople, at least the sales attitudes, they deserve.

Naturally, we all believe, like Professor Higgins in the well-known musical *My Fair Lady*, that we are mild, reasonable people with the milk of human kindness flowing by the litre in every vein but, to switch authors, 'to see ourselves as others see us' may reveal a different picture.

From schooldays, we are all familiar with some stereotypical behaviour: the aggressive playground bully, and the natural victim, the doormat. It is fairly obvious why the latter is unlikely to be an effective negotiator, but it is surprising how many people who are in their private lives fine, upstanding, compassionate and liberal citizens, and would never dream of browbeating their partners, their children or their gardeners, assume that the key to success in a business negotiation is to terrorize the opposing party into submission.

But most aggressive behaviour in negotiation is far from deliberate; it is typically a combination of bad habits which, like any habits, can be unlearned. Words we use thoughtlessly can appear arrogant or patronizing: an innocent phrase like 'Of course …' can come across as 'If you weren't an idiot you would know …', 'You should …' or 'you ought to …' may be intended as a helpful suggestion, but may suggest that you do not think the other party knows their job, and so on.

Surprisingly, though, the words we use are the least of the problem. Research (Mehrabian, 1981) shows that, typically, we only build about 7 per cent of our perception of another person from the words they use; 38 per cent comes from the tone of voice and 55 per cent from body language. (Many people disbelieve this, but the experiments are repeatable.) Also, body posture has a great influence on voice tone, partly explaining why negotiating on the telephone can be so unsatisfactory: although you cannot see the other party, if they are hunched over a small desk with the handset jammed under their chin, they can certainly come over as more aggressive and peremptory than they mean to.

Of course, aggression does sometimes work, at least in the short term – as a buyer, if your supplier is fool enough to send you the office trainee, or has mistakenly hired one of nature's lambs as a salesperson. But trainees mature, and lambs (or 'non-assertive personalities' in the jargon) do not last long. And people move around. Today's bullied salespersons who find themselves in a weak position may one day return in a situation where the power is reversed. If you have conditioned them to feel that hardball is the only way to negotiate, you may find yourself in an awkward position.

So there are entirely pragmatic, as well as ethical, reasons for trying not to be either a bully or a doormat. Treat your opposite party with respect, and you will be respected in return. Equally, self-respect engenders a positive response. The aim is for a behaviour that combines assertiveness, which puts over your needs and requirements clearly, without appearing to impose them, and responsiveness, listening and responding to what the other party is saying and offering. There is a strong case for suggesting that listening is the most important, and the most neglected, part of negotiating behaviour.

Cultivating assertive–responsive behaviour (Back and Back, 2005) increases the chances of your needs being met and is a crucial part of being able to retain control of a negotiation (it implies after all that you are in control of yourself). It does not, however, imply that there is only one style or approach to negotiation; in fact I identify five major styles to be used individually or, more profitably, in combination. Too many negotiators are 'one-club' players: they have a style that suits and which they believe, rightly or wrongly, to be effective, but they have not learnt to change their approach according to circumstances. This is also true of organizations who believe that their size guarantees the best result. I have been involved with many businesses and in over 30 years have rarely seen the lowest prices go to the largest volume customer (see Chapter 7).

If you completed the style profile questionnaire in the previous chapter, you will have a series of scores labelled A, C, B, T, L and E. Yes, there are six (Brown et al., 1966) (Figure 2.1)!

E is for Emotion

We all use emotion in domestic negotiations, but do not always recognize that it can be equally appropriate and powerful in the commercial arena. Yet every time we call on previous favours done, shared experiences, common interests (such as a love of a football club or a mutual desire to 'do down the opposition') or the prospect of future status and reward, we are playing on very basic human emotions, from loyalty to greed or even shame. Emotions are very powerful motivators and a score of 12 or more suggests that you understand this.

L is for Logic

This, of course, can be very powerful. If you can 'prove' that the other party's position is untenable, then surely they must make some concession? But what passes for logic can be grievously overused, especially perhaps by negotiators whose initial training was in science, engineering, accountancy or indeed some areas of law. Leaving aside the practical details – to win a logical argument you may have to know more about the other party's business and environment than they do themselves – a narrow reliance on logic ignores all the emotional and other human factors. A typical example: 'If you invest £x million in plant, we will give you all (rather than part) of our business. You will have lower unit costs, at least as good margins, guaranteed throughput and the prestige of being a preferred supplier to our blue-chip company.' Who could refuse? Well, actually, quite a lot of firms, who have, rationally or irrationally, a dislike of high debt levels, or having too much business in one basket, or may have had different plans for the way their firm is going. I recently came across an Australian company suggesting to a Japanese supplier a 5% discount for seven-day payments. This sounds good until you understand that borrowing money in Japan cost at the time about one-third of what it would in cost Australia. Logic can be a powerful style (and certainly, lack of logic is likely to be disastrous): scores of around 10 are appropriate.

T is for Threat

Not wishing to be aggressive, threats are often understated, sometimes barely voiced at all, and all the better for it. But suggestions that you are looking for alternative suppliers, that failure in this negotiation could impact on other contracts, that tolerance of slightly non-compliant practices may cease or that benefits may be withdrawn ('we would have to look again at whether you can cite us as a satisfied customer in your literature') do not need dictator-style banging of shoes on tables to hit home. 'Less is more' when using threat, and if you make an explicit threat you have to be prepared to follow through: suggesting that you are looking at other suppliers when everyone knows there are no alternatives is to weaken, not strengthen, your position. A score of 7 or 8, but not more, suggests a good, controlled use of threat.

B is for Bargaining

Bargaining is a much more complex style, involving the trading off of many factors or variables, and for a lot of people only this is 'real' negotiation. Ideally, each side offers variables that cost them little, but have higher value to the recipient (consider the Japanese/Australian example above), although this is not always possible. Certainly, for those who enjoy the cut and thrust, this can be the most personally rewarding style, but that is not to say that bargaining alone necessarily leads to the best resolution of the negotiation and so a score of around 8 is good.

C is for Compromise

Contrary to popular opinion, bargaining and compromise are not at all the same thing. Compromise is about seeking the middle ground or, often, splitting the difference (though not necessarily 50:50). Many details of a negotiation may come down to this, but it is a style to adopt only when other, more creative, techniques have failed to bridge the gap. Compromise is perhaps what computers would do if they could negotiate. And remember that the objective of a negotiation is to leave both sides feeling reasonably content, whereas very often, a compromise satisfies neither party. You are looking for a low score here, no more than 3.

A is for Acceptance

Everything is negotiable. All too often people exchange information, test understanding and then accept the status quo rather than negotiate. In some cultures and organizations acceptance is a preferred approach, less challenging and hence more comfortable. As I travel around the world, in some cities I will see a score of 0 for acceptance, which is correct; however, in some cities and organizations I will see a score of 3 or more, which is not desirable. I can usually predict where I will see a score of 3+, and in which cultures and organizations.

Summary

Puzzled? Why do we want to score highly on such a slippery subject as the regular use of emotion, but have our propensity to bargain apparently undervalued? Look again at the five approaches. They split into two quite different groups: emotion, logic and threat on the one side; bargaining and compromise on the other. The difference is fundamental: E, L and T do NOT have to cost your side anything. You do not have to make concessions or offer benefits, at least of a commercial nature: you are creating a condition in which the other party wants or needs to move towards your position without receiving anything tangible in return (except for the business itself). Bargaining and compromise, by contrast, both require you to offer or surrender some commercial value as well as receive: both parties have to move.

So it seems reasonable that in any negotiation process, we should start by employing some or all of the more manipulative styles – emotion, logic and threat – before hitting the nitty gritty of bargaining and, if all else fails, compromise. E, L and T can be regarded as a softening-up process or, as the sociologists prefer to describe it, 'conditioning'. In the next chapter we will look at how conditioning can begin to be applied well before formal negotiation commences.

But to use any of these styles (other than outright acceptance or straight 'split the difference' compromise) we need some raw material to work on. Logic requires research to make a case; using emotion or threat presupposes that you know where the opposing party may be persuaded; to bargain, there must be several, preferably many, factors or variables to bargain with: a negotiation with only one variable, such as unit price, is highly likely to end in stalemate,

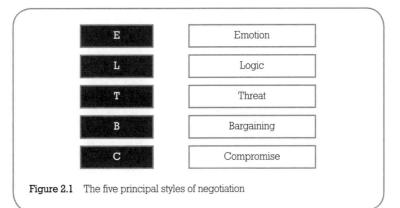

Figure 2.1   The five principal styles of negotiation

broken, if at all, by an unsatisfactory compromise. Determining the factors and variables, creating the raw material for a negotiation, is an essential part of the planning and preparation process.

As an introduction to the next chapter, consider one of your current or recent negotiations – as straightforward an example as possible (a year's supply of a single component, for example) – and make a couple of lists. In the first, list all the questions you might ask of your potential supplier/customer, all the information you might try to acquire. In the second, list all the variables that could conceivably be brought into the negotiation, by either party, and that are therefore available to trade. (A hint: both lists should be a lot longer than you initially think, even for the simplest deal. See also Figure 9.2 in Chapter 9.)

Remember

1. Be clear about your preferred style.
2. Be clear about the other party's preferred style: is it personally adopted or driven by your organization?
3. Try to move your style: do not be a 'one-club' player.

3

The Power of Planning

Time spent in reconnaissance is seldom wasted, as the great generals acknowledge.

Successful negotiators spend a lot of time and effort in planning their approach (Rackham and Carlisle, 1978), in research, and in preparing positions and tactics for a wide range of eventualities.

When considering buyer/seller negotiations, it must be admitted at the outset that the buyer is often at a disadvantage in this regard. Where a buyer may be responsible for the commercial relationship with dozens or even hundreds of suppliers, the salesperson or account manager may have the luxury of focusing on just a handful of buyers for perhaps just one product or service. What appears to the buyer to be a cold call may be the result of weeks or months of research by the vendor company. The latter, if they are doing their job right, may know almost as much about your firm, its business and its business environment as the buyer does. Except in the largest negotiations, buyers are unlikely to be able to be so single-minded in researching potential suppliers, but in any negotiation you owe it to yourself to find out what you can.

But planning and preparation are not just about information gathering. Objectives, strategies, tactics and the physical environment also need to be considered.

Aims and Objectives

The planning and preparation process starts with an aim. The aim may be to conclude an acceptable deal with this supplier or customer; it may equally, as a buyer, be to discover what the best available deal is so that it can be compared with those from other suppliers. Objectives are planned: the goals you must achieve to be able to call the negotiation successful. Objectives will be prioritized: some will be more important than others, and some may be alternatives; and in most cases objectives will be defined as a range of acceptable outcomes rather than a single value.

As a buyer planning a negotiation, you will need to work out your own position, in terms of supply positioning (Steele and Court, 1996), and make the best assumptions possible about the supplier's likely position (see Chapter 8). This will not only suggest appropriate strategies and tactics, but almost certainly reveal significant gaps in your knowledge. Always be wary of assumed knowledge, and make a clear distinction between what you know and what you only think you know.

Questions, Variables and Information

As in a military campaign, objectives, strategies and tactics are all very well, but you cannot fight without ammunition. At the end of the previous chapter I invited you to make a couple of lists, based on some relatively straightforward recent negotiation, of questions that you might raise in the 'testing' phase, and of variables that might come into play in the 'moving' phase. (I will explain these terms later, but they refer to recognizably distinct stages that any well-conducted negotiation will go through.) In both cases you should have a lot: a couple of dozen or more. You will not necessarily use them all, and some will be variations on a theme, different ways of arriving at the same point, but they constitute your ammunition, the raw material of negotiation. If you run out of ammunition, in effect you have surrendered control of the way the negotiation proceeds to the other party.

You cannot have enough questions or variables: you cannot have enough information either, and the more sources it is derived from the better (Rackham and Carlisle, 1978). For high-risk, high-value negotiations you may want to purchase specialist market intelligence and analysts' reports, but a lot of information is freely available, especially through searching the Internet. The negotiator's task here is certainly much easier than it was a few years ago. Annual reports and accounts are essential, while credit checks and other reports from agencies such as Dunn & Bradstreet can be very revealing (your sales ledger colleagues can probably help here). From a buying perspective, visits to suppliers can be very important, as can talking to other customers (preferably not just the few that are volunteered as satisfied clients). Any records and experience of previous negotiations with the firm should be tapped, and do not forget the human element: salespeople move around a lot, but often stay in the same general area of business, so it is quite possible that someone has dealt with the individual before, even if the company they represent is new to you.

Space, Time and Environment

There are other issues that need advance planning. The first is ensuring that the salesperson or buyer has a positive frame of mind when dealing with you. A salesperson or buyer may base this mindset on the impressions gathered in the first contact at the reception desk. Polite greeting and ensuring that the visitor is not kept waiting beyond the appointment time are but two factors that can have a significant influence. Remember that there is much to be gleaned about how the supplier/buyer views you from the way you are treated as a guest.

The physical environment also matters. Negotiators who are cramped, uncomfortable, cold, thirsty or having to balance papers on their knees are unlikely to give their best; indeed, they are likely to become uncooperative or aggressive. Background noise, telephone rings, constant interruptions or colleagues peering through windows does not help either. Remember to divert your calls and turn your mobile off.

Often there may be advantages in negotiating on neutral ground away from the inevitable distractions of the office or factory. A local hotel may be suitable, but beware that alcohol is a poor crutch for effective negotiation.

Sometimes it may be advantageous to meet in the other party's premises. This is of special value to buyers, who have the opportunity to check for themselves the validity of the claims about stock availability, level of used capacity and excellence of facilities.

The time factor needs to be considered too. Few people perform at their best against deadlines, and the last half-hour on a Friday afternoon is unlikely to show either side at their best in a negotiation of any complexity. Often, it can be predicted that a negotiation will take more than one meeting, so you need to set interim objectives for what needs to have been raised or achieved at each meeting. In Chapter 7 I will refer to a major intergovernment negotiation that took 19 months and many meetings.

Whether you expect to conclude business in a single meeting, or a whole series of encounters, a negotiation moves through distinct phases. There is a preparation and planning phase, an opening, a testing or discovery phase, a moving phase, a closing or agreement phase and a review phase. I will look at each of these in detail in subsequent chapters, but each phase should be planned and prepared for in advance.

However, beware of building up a rigid sequential plan. 'I will ask him question A, thus exposing the weakness of his case; he will offer X, I will hold out for Y and encourage him by offering Z which does not cost me anything, and we will sign at 4.35' may be very convincing in front of the bathroom mirror, but things are never that simple. Your opposite number may have some completely new proposal you never anticipated; or may agree instantly to some point that you thought would be difficult to win, but be unexpectedly reluctant to make what you imagined would be a relatively minor concession elsewhere. The point of planning and preparation is to increase your flexibility and responsiveness, not to constrain it.

For the same reason it is not usually a good idea to invest much in set-piece speeches, presentations and 'death by PowerPoint'. We are all too familiar with the double-glazing rep or telesales operative who cannot manage anything that departs from the planned or computer-prompted spiel; but buyers' responses can be equally formulaic. And if you are concentrating on delivering a set piece, or a rehearsed line of argument, you are almost certainly not listening to what is really going on in the negotiation, and the unanticipated offers and opportunities will pass you by.

Teamwork

Another factor that needs forethought is the question of whether the negotiation is to be carried out by a single individual (and if so, who?) or by a team. A number of influences may be at work here: the size, nature or complexity of a purchase or sale may require the presence of functional specialists, for example. Different user groups may insist on being present. If the vendor is likely to be fielding several people, strict parity of numbers is not essential, but it can be hard and lonely work being a sole negotiator against a team. Cultural influences may obtrude: in Japanese companies, for example, negotiation between teams is the norm (even if most team members remain silent), and one-on-one negotiating may be regarded as worryingly individualistic. Even if you are proposing to negotiate solo there may be advantages in having a colleague present to take notes.

Managing a negotiating team is an art in itself. There are many examples of highly successful team negotiation, where individuals complement each other's skills, forming a well-understood division of labour together with a detailed understanding and agreement about the objectives and the strategies to be deployed. However, there are many examples where poor teamwork has been disastrous.

Beware of, and if possible avoid, the following: the chairman or senior board member ('I'll just sit at the back and observe') who is bound to be appealed to over the head of the lead negotiator, whose subsequent authority to negotiate the deal will be reduced to close to zero. Indeed, encourage the other side to include their managing director (or similar), for if they can be manoeuvred to agree to your position who can overrule them? Organizations that have thought about their negotiations and have trained for them would always keep the MD or other senior directors out of the way to use 'defence in depth' (see Chapter 11 on Tactics and Ploys). Also avoid technical types whose enthusiasm for specific features can blind them to the commercial realities; end-users, especially minor end-users, who cannot see why their own detailed requirement is not the centrepiece of the whole negotiation; and anyone who is likely to lose concentration and then reopen an issue that has already been settled, skip to a completely unrelated point or volunteer vital information that you have been at pains to conceal from the other side. Some teams are adept and skilled at spotting and exploiting the fracture lines in an opposing team.

If you have to work with a team, and sometimes it is unavoidable, it is essential that everybody understands who is in charge, what their own responsibilities and contributions are, how their own particular concerns are being addressed and, crucially, how to keep their mouths shut. If at all possible, bring the team together before the meeting and rehearse them in the major points and how the negotiation is likely to proceed. The importance of stage managing cannot be overemphasized, for all too often have I seen disaster created from success by someone concentrating on what they wanted to say and not listening to the negotiation.

There is another aspect to preparation, and that is conditioning. Conditioning covers all the methods you can use to modify the other party's expectations. Conditioning runs right through the negotiation process, but it should start well before any meeting. As a preparation for the next chapter, try to think of ways in which, looking from a buyer's view, you could influence a potential vendor's view of you and your business needs, before you ever meet.

Remember

1. Preparation and planning are not just about information gathering. It is about *how* you are going to do what you are going to do as much as, if not more than, the task itself.
2. You should have a range of outcomes and objectives.
3. Have a comprehensive list of variables.
4. There is no such thing as a foolish question, hence do not feel embarrassed to ask.
5. You may need more than one meeting.
6. Stage-manage teams.

4

The Opening and Conditioning

Impatience is never a virtue.

With all preparation done, objectives clear, arguments rehearsed, facts at fingertips and a laptop full of back-up, the urge to get on with the negotiation, to 'cut to the chase', as they say in another context, after the most perfunctory of preliminaries, can be almost irresistible.

But resisted it must be. A well-conducted negotiation goes through a number of distinct phases before any trade-offs are made: ignore or skip these, and the resulting deal, if it happens at all, is almost bound to be suboptimal.

The face-to-face negotiation will move through an opening, then a period of exploration or testing, to a phase of movement (which is where the bargaining and trading largely occur, although many other things are also going on, as you will see in the next chapter), and finally a closure. Too many executives charged with negotiating a deal focus on phase three (movement) and regard the rest as mere formality or window-dressing; but they are wrong. The opening and testing phases *condition* the whole basis of any negotiation, while a failure to close the deal properly can lead to confusion and disaster.

Conditioning – that word again. Conditioning covers all the methods you can use to predispose the other party towards your wishes and position. At the end of the previous chapter I suggested that you think of ways in which you can condition the other party; that is, change their expectations of what they can hope for from any deal, before the meeting even starts. Conditioning does not cease with the first handshake – almost everything you do throughout a negotiation is in part aimed at altering hopes and expectations (not necessarily just of the current deal), but it starts a long time before. As I have written elsewhere, 'If you're thinking about when to start a negotiation it may already be too late ... It is never too early to begin in terms of conditioning the other party, shaping their expectations or creating a powerful first impression. The end of your next negotiation could be the beginning of the one after' (Steele and Beasor, 1999).

Since negotiation is a two-way process, your opposite number is trying to condition you at the same time. Nonetheless, there is a first mover advantage, or 'getting your retaliation in first' as a famous sports commentator used to say. A vendor who asks for a meeting to renegotiate a price, for example, is likely to mutter darkly about world commodity prices, the climate change levy or other factors that are designed to do two things: to assure you that there is little room for manoeuvre to counteract these external factors (which naturally are affecting the competition as well) and to accustom you to the idea of say a 10 per cent increase, so that when the rep offers 'only' a 5 per cent increase you positively swoon with gratitude. You know the feeling.

But as a buyer you too need to get your conditioning in: veiled references to other quotations, alternative sources or new technologies; suggestions that you just know they will be fascinated to learn more about your inventory reduction plan/vendor rating scheme or your concern at the weakness in the market are examples of counters that you really need to deploy. If you are initiating the negotiation it is that much easier to commence conditioning. Consider, for example, as a buyer how a vendor will react to:

(a) a formal Request for Quotation with considerable supporting documentation and signed by the director of purchasing

(b) a voicemail suggesting that the supplier 'drops by sometime – I've some business to discuss that you might be able to assist us with'.

Of course, there is no single 'right' answer. A lot depends on the previous history of the business relationship, the degree of understanding between the people involved, and what you are trying to achieve. For example, (a) probably implies 'this is really important to us – we want your best people, your best proposals, and you are up against some blue-chip competition', whereas (b) might be understood as 'this is fairly trivial and I don't want to waste too much time: don't give me the PowerPoint presentation, I just want a keen price'. Alternatively and depending on the conditions, there may be the implication that while this job is nothing in itself, a useful response could lead to greater things. However, it could give the impression that you are not bothering with competitive quotes and the job is as good as won; that is probably not the sort of conditioning you are aiming for.

So a negotiation can start sooner than you think. This point is best illustrated with a real-world example.

Devaluation

A Swiss engineering company fell victim to a wild fluctuation in currency values. At that time such was the appreciation of the Swiss franc in relation to sterling that it needed to increase its prices to its UK customers and others around the world by 35 per cent just to preserve its profit margins. Many companies would have given up. The situation seemed impossible!

Would you believe that a company could increase its prices by a large amount in a highly competitive market and still survive?
I knew that with some careful negotiation, and some detailed planning work behind the scenes, it could be pulled off. In a nutshell, the story went as follows: the company's first move was to look at its own costs, buying stock and currency forward, buying raw materials for its parent company. Having made all the savings it could, it still required a 20 per cent rise in its selling price into the UK market to preserve margins.

I prepared a detailed strategy with their sales team. The sales manager telephoned all his major customers in the UK to talk to their respective buyers about the 35 per cent movement in relative currency values. Using a prepared briefing, the sales manager talked around the subject, talked about some of the problems this created for his own company, and kept emphasizing the 35 per cent.[2] Avoiding the temptation, he said nothing about increasing prices.

His next step was to take most of his big UK customers out to dinner. He took the opportunity to talk to them about the recent currency fluctuation, always referring to the 35 per cent movement.

Although the company had identified savings which between them meant that a 20 per cent price increase would maintain current margins, it decided to 'posture' at 24 per cent with a detailed supporting outline.

His UK customers were household name companies in highly competitive markets. Despite that and in response to the sales manager's indirect approach, 11 of these companies contacted him saying they would accept a 35 per cent price increase: 'no one can be held responsible for currency movements'.

This was before he had asked for an increase, and was well above what he planned to ask for!

So some weeks after the initial telephone call and the discussions over dinner, the sales manager wrote to his other customers requesting a

---

2   Refer to Chapter 11 on Tactics – Broken Record.

24 per cent price increase. A total of 13 customers agreed to pay the 24 per cent increase, while some negotiated lower increases.

The net result was that the average increase achieved from more than 40 UK customers (most of which were among the country's top 200 ranking companies) was in excess of 25 per cent. As a consequence, the Swiss company *increased* its margins.

Negotiations can begin before we realize it, perhaps with a casual telephone call through which another party can indirectly implant an idea, conditioning our behaviour.

Conditioning carries on, even intensifies, in the opening face-to-face phase of the negotiation proper. Everything about your organization says something to the trained observer (and you have to assume that your counterpart has been trained). Ergo, everything can be used to convey a message and to condition expectations. (If you are the visitor to their premises, then you should be training yourself to pick up both deliberate and unconscious messages from them.)

But assume for the moment that you are a buyer and that you are the host. What do you want the salesperson or negotiator to feel like? There are two key messages, regardless of context, that you should be putting across: that you are personally warm and that you are professionally tough.

Warm but Tough

This can appear contradictory, but actually warm and tough are points on different axes (Figure 4.1). By 'warm', we mean that you and the organization you represent want to come over as friendly, honest, open to ideas and suggestions, respectful of the other party as a fellow professional, and of the organization he or she represents as a serious entity. 'Liking' or 'friendship' is an optional extra; think rather in terms of 'respect', but at the same time you need to put over the 'tough' message: you and your organization are not to be trifled with, you have goals and requirements that will be satisfied one way or another, you are not the sort of person who can be seduced by some minor concession or conned into a false position. Warm and tough are not contradictory; they are mutually supportive: if your opposite number views you as open, honest and well disposed, he or she is more likely to believe you when you lay out your position. If, however, you are seen as cold, hostile, secretive and devious, that inevitably discourages the other party from looking for a cooperative solution, and may even create a mindset in which they aim to take you for every short-term gain they can get, or perhaps just to walk away.

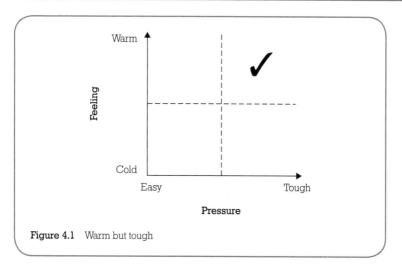

Figure 4.1   Warm but tough

Many years ago I designed a business game, entitled *The Property Developer*. I, together with colleagues, have used this game in negotiation training programmes thousands of times. Part of the wrap-up analysis involves asking team members how they feel about other teams. This is undertaken before the winning team is known. My records, over many years, show that the winning team can be identified most of the time by finding the team that exhibits a higher incidence of warm and tough, as viewed by other teams, together with a high clarity of objective.

So the opening phase of any negotiation is critical in establishing your 'warm and tough' criteria, while at the same time starting or continuing the conditioning process. What does this mean in practice?

First Impressions

First impressions are important and that means your reception. Make your opposite number park two hundred yards away across a building site, have your receptionist mispronounce his name or spend five minutes confirming his appointment, leave him on a hard bench without a coffee for half an hour after the booked time for the meeting, and see just how eager to please even the most desperate person will be! Do as you would be done by is a sound precept in negotiation.

But, also, use this period positively, to give or withhold information. For example, the pegboard with 'Acme Holdings welcomes John Smith of Grunge Widgets' is a nice touch. Leaving up the names of the other firms in contention may be a useful ploy, if you feel the need to concentrate your visitor's mind. Sometimes you may not wish your visitor to be aware of the competition, and your receptionist should be able to 'lose' the signing-in book for half an hour or so!

Digging a hole!

A large excavator company decided to outsource its security. They struck a low-cost deal which impacted on the pay and conditions of the actual security guards.

A few weeks into the new security arrangements along came one of their largest customers, a self-made millionaire on an unannounced visit. His gleaming red Rolls-Royce was turned away at the security gate with the words 'Sorry mate, visitor car park is full, you will have to park down the road – 200/300 metres away and I can't lift the barrier, you will have to turn in the road.' Five minutes later, parked at the side of the road, the client rang the sales director and informed him that all future orders would be passed to their main competitor. An emotional reaction which the self-made person may have regretted but never changed.

If all this seems a little theatrical, that is deliberate. You are creating what thespians call a *mise-en-scène*, and detail is vital. The message must be consistent: if you are about to plead poverty, do not have some lad polishing the chairman's Jag outside! Equally, if your 'come-on' is the prospect of increasing future business, hide the announcement that the staff Christmas party has been cancelled as an economy measure! You get the picture.

Opening the Meeting

This conditioning or scene-setting continues into the meeting itself. As discussed in the last chapter, you will have given thought to the physical environment: friendly and relaxed but at the same time businesslike and professional.

The social niceties are not merely to be skipped through. Introductions and chit-chat give you (both) a chance to see the other in a relatively relaxed condition: a norm. If behaviour changes later, that tells you something. There is a lot of useful information you can glean in five or ten minutes at the beginning, which may be exploited later: shared interests or common ground, general views on economic and commercial conditions, and especially if the person or the firm is new to you, a lot of background which will flesh out and modulate your own research.

Do not ignore the ritual exchange of business cards, which is particularly important in some cultures. You have probably assumed that the person you are meeting is in a position to make authoritative offers and decisions; it is not necessarily so, especially with bland job titles like 'business development executive', which could imply anything from office junior to commissioned agent. Indeed, I once met an assistant buyer who was actually the deputy MD: the helicopter collecting him gave it away! But people are very touchy about status; it can be much easier to assess their real power and position in these informal preliminary moments than if the issue arises later in formal talks.

The status and authority of your opposite number is just one assumption that you will have made, and now need to question. In fact, a large part of your preparation for this meeting is probably based on assumptions; but do you know what is assumption and what is fact? How are you going to test this? In the next chapter we will look at this centrally important 'testing' phase. But remember *conditioning*. There is no such thing as a free lunch. To quote from a research study:

'Business negotiations with a customer are more PRODUCTIVE in a relaxed atmosphere' (McCracken and Callahan, 1996).

Remember

1. Negotiations go through a number of distinct phases.
2. A negotiation can start sooner than you think.
3. Conditioning carries on throughout the negotiation.
4. Try to achieve a warm and professionally tough approach.
5. Be clear about the other party's status and authority.

5

Assumptions and Questions

ASS U ME
Remember assumptions will make an ass of you and me!

If you have followed me so far, you will have got the message that assumptions are some of the most dangerous things in a negotiation. You could even buy the wrong London Bridge as one American allegedly once did.

Both parties to a negotiation necessarily come to the table with a variety of assumptions, all of which have to be tested. You, for example, have probably assumed that the person you are meeting has the power to conclude the deal; hopefully you have already explored that particular one during the opening courtesies (Chapter 4). We hope you have not made too many limiting or constraining assumptions, for example that a particular element of, or route to, a potential deal 'isn't worth' exploring because the other party 'would never accept it'. You may well be right, but you do not know that until you have asked. (That is acceptance, which we decided in Chapter 2 has no place as a negotiating style.) Never assume that something is impossible; in negotiation, all routes are open until a definitive roadblock has been put up (and even a categorical 'No' is not always final) (refer to Scenario 11, Chapter 13).

You will necessarily, though, have made other important assumptions, about, for example, how your supplier or potential supplier views you and your business (see Chapter 8). It may be obvious to you that you are this firm's most important and valued customer or supplier, but you cannot be sure of that until you have tested the hypothesis.

Similarly, as a buyer, you may feel entitled to assume that the other party has interpreted your Request for Quotation, or whatever, in the sense in which you wrote it. This may not be so, and you must both test out your assumption and allow the other side to test theirs. A simple example: you are inviting quotes to establish a second source of supply, for increased security. The vendor is likely, if he or she has done her homework, to have a good idea of your total demand, and may assume that that whole volume is available, and be

33

bidding on that basis. You really do need to know at an early stage if that is the case.

The whole conditioning process described in the previous chapter is instrumental in modifying and correcting assumptions and expectations. Conditioning can work both ways: as a buyer you can condition the vendor to be grateful for the scraps from your table, or to expect and really work for the whole 12-course banquet.

Testing means questioning; but asking questions (and just as crucially, listening to the answers) is of far more importance than merely eliciting information and testing assumptions. Asking questions (along with actively listening to the response or reaction, and summarizing at frequent intervals) helps you to take and retain control of the pace and direction of a negotiation (or indeed of any other meeting).

For many people this is counter-intuitive. Surely, it is the person doing the talking who is in control, who 'has the stage', who won't let you get a word in edgeways? Well, if you are determined to be a doormat that may be so. But provided you have practised assertive (not aggressive) and responsive behaviours (see Chapter 2) then your questioning will set the agenda and decide where the negotiation goes.

Why is this? There are a number of reasons, but the most important concerns the flow of information. Information, it is generally agreed, is power. Every time you open your mouth in a meeting you are liable to give information away, deliberately or accidentally. Every time you keep quiet and let the other person talk you will receive, if you listen and look (remember body language), a wealth of information, some of it unintended. However, effective listening is not as easy as you may think (see Chapter 10).

Try the following listening test on a friend. Read it to them and see how they get on.

Listening test

You are the leader of a search party looking for a plane which has crashed in the wilderness. After searching the area for some time you eventually locate deep furrows made by the plane as it crash landed. Following the furrows you see the plane, with its back broken, lying partially submerged in the middle of a river. There is no obvious sign of life. You realize there is no way you can carry the dead back to civilization and you must choose where to bury them. It would be easier to get them to the far bank but the ground is very rocky. To bring them to the near bank would be much more difficult because of the depth of the water and the speed of the current, but once on the bank the job will be relatively easy as the ground is relatively soft.

> On which side of the river – the near or far side – would you bury the
> survivors? Read this question quickly and see what answers you get
> from your friends.

And if you cannot think of the right question or response, say
nothing! Silence is incredibly powerful. There is a human instinct
to leap into the breach, fill the gap, and so people start babbling.
Readers who 'enjoyed' interviews with old-fashioned head
teachers will know what we mean: silent reproach can be far more
demoralizing than any amount of rant or reason. Indeed, silence can
be sufficiently intimidating for me to counsel against its overuse in
negotiations where preserving a good relationship is important. Ask
your spouse or significant other if you do not believe me.

A silent rector
A good friend of mine held the post of rector in a large parish church
in England. At Remembrance Sunday service each November he held
the traditional two-minute silence but because he never wore a watch
the silence never lasted more than the record-breaking 58 seconds!
Silences are long even when there is no pressure on.

Open and Closed Questions

Not all questions are good questions. Except where the question is
purely a request for information, avoid 'closed' questions. A closed
question is one that invites a short, sharp answer, typically 'Yes'
or 'No'. They have an attraction for barristers, because they leave
the witness with nowhere to go. 'Did you speak to the defendant
on the night of the 24th? ... I remind you, you are on oath.' But
closed questions can come back to bite us, and may leave the whole
negotiation with nowhere to go. The classic questions to avoid are
those along the lines of 'Is that your final offer?' or 'Is this your best
price?'

He or she has to say 'Yes', in which case that is the end of the
negotiation and it is accept or reject time. What does the buyer here
expect the vendor to say? 'No, I've got lots more; I'm just trying it
on'?

A closed question closes off an avenue of enquiry, or even a whole
deal. An open question tries to open new ways of reaching the goal.
Fortunately, only a little thought and awareness are needed to turn
a closed question into an open one. 'Do you have the capacity to
manufacture 5000 units a month?' is a closed question: 'Yes', and the
deal lives; 'No' and you have a problem. Ask instead, 'How would you

achieve the capacity for 5000 a month?' and you immediately open up alternatives, proposals and counter-proposals.

Also, and reverting to an earlier point, questions that require the other party to explain and expound get them talking, and therefore giving information. However, do be a little wary of 'Why?' questions. They invite the other party to deliver a totally logical explanation of why something must be just so and the logic may be unassailable, at least with the time and information at your disposal. Logic is a powerful persuader – for both sides.

The testing out of some assumptions is a necessary preliminary to serious attempts to move the other party's position, although in reality testing and moving is an iterative process: you probe some aspect of the deal, move things as far as you can at that time, use an adroit question to shift the focus, probe again, move again, and so on. At every stage it is invaluable to summarize.

Summarizing

This is not only because life can get confusing when, as often happens, there are several alternative conditional (i.e. 'If you do X then I'll offer Y') offers on the table. Presenting a summary is another way of asserting control of the negotiation. If you are doing the summarizing, you can convert a tentative suggestion into an almost agreed element of the deal; equally, you can quietly ignore less attractive proposals or elements.

Of course, the other party is free to dispute your summary, but if they do not, their tacit acceptance will make it much harder to revisit and renegotiate these points later on. For the same reason, if a negotiation is discontinuous, it is an excellent idea to put down your version of the plot so far in an email or a fax to the other side. Do not actively solicit their agreement, as that just encourages them to rethink and renege, besides which it may turn out to be you that wants to revisit a particular point later; but if the other side does not quibble, then you have a secure foundation for the next phase of negotiation.

All the time, through repeated questioning, listening and summarizing, we are seeking to move the other party through the judicious use of the five great persuaders (negotiation styles): emotion, logic, threat, bargaining and compromise, in that order of preference.

It is easy to see how questions can address bargain and compromise: typically, hypothetical questions with 'If … then …'. But questions can also be framed to exploit those cost-free persuaders: emotion, logic and threat. Questions starting, 'How do you feel about ...?', 'Where do you see us going ...?' and so on can, especially in a relationship-heavy negotiation, draw the other party into almost an emotional conspiracy (and encourage them to give even more information). Being asked for your opinions is always flattering. By contrast, 'Wouldn't it be a shame if ...?' is a nice, warm-but-tough, way of veiling a threat.

Whatever combination of persuaders we use, eventually we will reach a position where the deal on the table looks about as good as it's reasonably going to get. So: a handshake and a coffee while the contracts people knock out the legalese, and then on to the next deal? Not so fast. There is still work to do, as we shall see in the next chapter. For more detail on questioning and listening see Chapter 10.

Remember

1. Test your assumptions: they are dangerous.
2. Learn different types of questions.
3. Focus on listening and getting information.

6

Concluding the Deal and Analysing the Process

'Fools rush in …', to quote from a famous song.

When someone offers you their hand, the natural reaction, at least in the West, is to reach out and shake it. As professionals, of course, we are steeled against accepting the first, or even the 21st offer that comes along; nonetheless, at some point the negotiation will have progressed as far as can reasonably be hoped for without disproportionate time and effort being expended for decreasing returns, and if what is on the table is acceptable to both parties, then why not shake on it? It's a deal!

Hang on. What deal? Or, very often, which deal? Most negotiations go through phases where there are competing proposals or alternative solutions on the table. Each side, naturally, tries to 'pick'n'mix' the most attractive features. The result is that, unless the handshake is over a clear and agreed summary, there is a very high risk that each side believes it has agreed to a different deal, or that the deal struck contains mutually incompatible elements.

There was a nice illustration of this danger a few years ago, when the professional footballers in the UK were in dispute over the allocation of income from TV rights. After an acrimonious (and very badly run) negotiation, both sides emerged separately to face the cameras. 'We've settled: we've won £60 million', said the footballers; 'We've settled, it's cost us £50 million', the proprietors proclaimed. Unsurprisingly, they were soon back at the table, and with an even worse relationship than before.

It is tempting to believe that you have agreement on the broad issues and that the details will somehow all come out in the wash, or on the exchange of contracts. This is dangerous: not only are one side's minor details frequently of vital importance to the other, but many negotiations either do not go to a formal contract, or imply one side or the other taking action in advance of contract. If, for example, as a buyer, your handshake has left your supplier with the impression that they have won the whole order, and they had better tool up for that immediately, the subsequent discovery that you thought you had explained you were only offering half the business is not going to make them happy. Verbal contracts in many countries are still contracts and, however difficult they may be to prove in court, court is just where this sort of misunderstanding tends to end up, with a substantial cost to the parties involved.

So: always shake on an agreed summary, and exchange that in writing as soon as possible thereafter. It is also important to write up your notes, as near contemporaneously as possible, not just or even principally as a legal protection, but as a way of learning and improving.

How Well Did I Do?

Negotiation skills can and should be practised and honed throughout life. One does not want to get into the Korean mindset (see Chapter 12 on negotiating globally); Koreans, according to an article in *The Economist*, '… approach all talks as a zero sum game. Any agreement, by this logic, means they have conceded too much …' At the same time, there is no such thing as a perfect negotiation: even if you obtain all your objectives, there may have been something else you could have tried for; and even more likely, there could have been a better, simpler, less abrasive, more pleasurable (to both parties) way of getting there.

If from the buying office you could see the salesperson who has just left you sitting in the company car in your car park, or heading back out to the motorway, you would probably see them either scribbling notes or talking to themselves. Good salespeople are trained to debrief themselves: they make mental or physical notes about customers and their company; facts they have learnt that could be useful in future (ranging from 'Buyer a staunch teetotaller: don't suggest drink after meeting' to 'Visitor's book suggests they are talking to our biggest competitor: I need greater room to move'). They will also be reviewing their strategy and tactics: Were you impervious to an implied threat of ceasing supply? Were you easily drawn into and convinced by a purely logical argument? Did you appear to be under pressure and easy meat for a compromise just to get the business off your desk? And so on.

Everyone should review what went right, and what went wrong. In this review phase you should be considering the following questions. Which were the sucker punches you fell for? Were you in control – how did you find yourself discussing volumes when you had been determined to save that for a later meeting? Were you properly prepared? Why had you completely misguessed the other side's view of your business? And particularly, review the meeting or the deal against the aims and objectives you had set beforehand. Were they credible and appropriate? Were they achievable? Were they achieved?

Some firms are investing heavily in supplier relationship management and customer relationship management systems in which a lot of detail on a negotiation can be logged systematically and be available for future use. A word of caution, though: personal details about salespeople or buyers and others with whom you negotiate are to be kept highly confidential, otherwise the data protection legislation could turn round and bite you. But you do not need fancy systems to conduct a systematic review of your negotiation and to learn lessons for next time.

Four Pillars of Negotiation

Negotiation is not checklist driven: it needs to be flexible and adaptable. Nonetheless, beneath the deliberately descriptive, rather than analytical, language I have used there lies a solid structure. I call this the 'four pillars' of negotiation (Figure 6.1), and it provides a useful framework in which to carry out your review and plan your need for self-improvement or, conceivably, for external training.

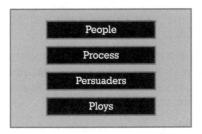

Figure 6.1 The four pillars of negotiation

The four pillars are people, process, persuaders and ploys (Figure 6.1). Remember that negotiation is carried out essentially between human beings, not between corporations, and some of the questions you should be asking yourself include:

People

■ How far did I display value and respect for the other party as a person? Did they appear to value me? If not, why not?

- How well was I communicating? Was I talking the same language? Was I clear when I needed to be clear? Was I listening acutely to what the other person was really saying? Was I listening to what I was saying? Was I talking too much and giving information for free?

- How was my behaviour? Was I being aggressive or supine? If so, was this for a reason, because it was appropriate (and sometimes it may be), or had I just fallen into default mode?

Process

You should be asking yourself:

- Were my aims and objectives appropriate? Were preparation and planning adequate? How accurate were my views on our position and that of our counterpart?

- Did the opening set the right mood for the meeting? Did I test out all the assumptions I had made? Were there any nasty surprises? What does that say about the assumptions I made? Did I convey well what I needed from a deal? How well and early did I discover what the other side really wanted?

- How well did I control the course of negotiations? How effective was my questioning? How acute was my listening? How decisive were my summaries?

- How well did I work the trading of concessions? Was I getting value for whatever I offered? Was I giving away too much at once? Was I getting more value than I was giving away and therefore taking cost out for my organization?

- Did I spot the conclusion coming? How clear are both sides as to what has been concluded?

Persuaders (Negotiation Styles)

Your assessment of how you used emotion, logic, threat, bargaining and compromise is inevitably subjective, and it can be difficult looking back to be sure just what caused movement in the other party. But you should check what you believe worked against the approach you set out, and in particular, whether you got full value from the cost-free use of emotion, logic and threat before and during any bargaining and compromise. Use the simple plan shown in Figure 6.2 and complete one of these for what you thought would be the approaches at the planning phase and another for what actually

Us		Them
	E	
	L	
	T	
	B	
	C	

Figure 6.2   Use of persuaders

happened when you review the negotiation, either part-way through or at the conclusion.

Ploys

Tactics, stratagems, dodges or whatever you care to call them have been deliberately underplayed so far. There are as many of these as you like, and while some are of universal application, many are, to put it mildly, manipulative, which is why there are pages of them in many training manuals. As such, they have their place in a short-term 'winner takes all' negotiation, and certainly the buyer needs to be able to spot when they are being used on him or her; but they should be used with caution and deliberation in any negotiation where the ongoing relationship matters. The appropriate use of tactics and ploys, and of the counters to them, comes with practice and certainly you should replay mentally instances you come across, and analyse why and in what circumstances they were successful, or not. (See Chapter 11 for details on tactics.)

In the end, though, the most successful ploys for you, as with other aspects such as your behavioural patterns, will tend to be those with which you are most comfortable.

Raising your Game

Negotiation skills training is not some Californian cult aimed at changing the inner you (despite some similarities of terminology); rather, it is about helping negotiators to feel confident in using a wider repertoire more effectively and more appropriately to each situation. Most negotiators without any training naturally do many of the things I have talked about at least some of time: increased negotiation skills come from increased self-knowledge, self-awareness and self-control on which we can build to improve our control over the process and outcome of negotiations.

Self-awareness can be hard to come by, especially when it comes to looking at things like your own body language, or listening to your own tone of voice: it is a commonplace that people do not recognize their own voices on tape, and sometimes themselves on video or DVD! Regrettably, it is rarely appropriate to video 'live' commercial negotiations. If you are fortunate enough to work within a tight and self-confident group, there is no substitute for open and honest mutual criticism, but not everyone can take that exposure in the workplace; and of course many negotiators, especially in sales and purchasing, are necessarily working alone much of the time. A lot can also be learned about how you come across to others (as opposed to how you think you come across) by talking to close friends and family members, although again this requires a certain level of self-confidence.

Alternatively, negotiation skills training in a safe environment is available from a number of sources, typically combining theory with extensive role-play and other exercises. These almost always give even experienced negotiators fresh insights into their own and others' behaviour but, whether you go for formal training or not, the real key to improving your negotiation performance is an understanding of the subject, then practice, practice, practice!

Want to understand more? Then Part 2 awaits those who …

'Make time to grow, then to experience after learning: then adapt and change'.

Remember

1. Do not rush to conclusion; make a clear record of the fully comprehensive agreed summary.
2. Write the summary down.
3. Review the four pillars and make notes for next time.

Part 2

7

Know the Rules

Without Rules – Chaos!

In Part 1 I looked at the five basic approaches that negotiators use to generate movement. To recap, negotiation is a process through which parties move from their initially divergent positions to a point where agreement may be reached.

The five styles/persuaders are:

C   compromise

B   bargaining

T   threat/coercion

L   logical reasoning

E   emotion.

That is not an order of merit. As we will see in Chapter 8, there may be an odd occasion when a simple compromise, for example, is the most effective strategy given the objectives of the negotiation. There will be other occasions on which it is definitely a last resort – or perhaps not allowable at all!

Recall that two of these approaches, compromise and bargaining, are what I call 'two-way movers'; implicitly, both sides have to surrender some perceived advantage or benefit. But the other three, threat/coercion, emotion and logic, are 'one-way movers'; if you use them judiciously, you can gain from the other side without yourself surrendering anything.

Perhaps for that very reason to many people, especially in the Anglo-Saxon economies, compromise and bargaining are seen as fair means to reaching agreement. They see them as legitimate approaches. In contrast, coercion, emotion and logical reasoning, which are not so well understood in the UK and the USA, are often regarded as underhand or manipulative approaches. This is an unfortunate attitude which can leave a negotiator working with one hand behind his back. This and other points are illustrated in several case studies below.

All five styles or persuaders are considered in turn here, together with some simple rules suggesting when and how each should be used.

Compromise

There are many things shared by English-speaking peoples, one of which is a propensity to compromise. That they commonly confuse the terms negotiation and compromise, seeing them as synonymous, is just a reflection of their view on the world. Agreements are reached by compromising. Are there any other ways?

Compromise is popular because it seems a fair way to reach a settlement, because both parties seem to move roughly equal amounts. A similar perception is held about bargaining: that it is a reasonable way to reach agreement.

The compromiser, who believes that agreement is to be found on the middle ground, uses ploys like:

- 'Let's meet each other halfway.'

- 'Let's split the difference between what I want and what you want.'

Your PA wants a day off, but you've got so much work on you tell her (or him) it is impossible. You discuss the matter quickly and agree she will take a half-day. You have met in the middle, each getting exactly half of what you wanted. A compromise was, after all, the easiest way to reach agreement.

Compromising is quick and is often used to break a deadlock in a negotiation. It is unimaginative, however, and can result in you giving away more than you needed to, more than the other party would have been prepared to accept.

Compromise is not the same thing as bargaining. People compromise over a single issue (or variable), along a single dimension (price, for example), whereas they bargain over several issues (or variables), making trade-offs between, say, price and delivery, and payment terms and exclusivity. Negotiators give and take: a higher price for a quicker delivery; a discount for early settlement. But because compromise is across a single dimension, it is clearly easier to *value* concessions made during compromise. This may blind negotiators to the benefits of other available aspects of the deal, some of which may be hard to quantify, especially in cash terms.

Obviously, then, if two parties set out to find a compromise on one issue, the one that takes the more extreme position is likely to come out on top (Figure 7.1). For example, if your PA wanted a day off, she might be sufficiently astute to ask for two days off. That way she knows that when you meet her halfway, she will get the day she wanted.

Rule one of compromise: **Try to take an extreme but credible posture**. When the PA asked for twice the time off she wanted, her posture was extreme, but it was still credible. Similarly, a buyer looking for a 5 per cent discount may be more likely to get it by asking for 10 per cent rather than simply stating a 5 per cent target.

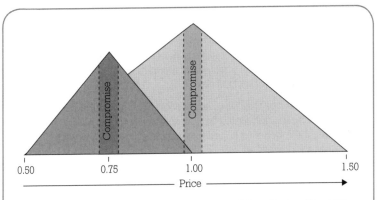

Figure 7.1 If a buyer is offering 0.5 per widget, and the seller is asking 1.00, the compromise will fall around 0.75. However, if the seller asks 1.50, the compromise will fall around 1.00. Compromise favours the person who takes the more extreme position, but it needs to be realistic!

Rule two of compromise: **Only use compromise as a last resort**. Try to find out more about the other party and to explore other approaches if possible. Imagine you are negotiating with someone you have not dealt with before. You have hardly begun and he suggests a compromise: 'Let's meet in the middle', he says. You are then faced with several questions: Is he a poor negotiator? Is he short of time and using compromise to force a quick agreement? Has he taken an extreme position, knowing he will benefit most from compromising? You do not know the answer to these questions so you should decline his invitation to compromise ... but not with a 'No'. Thank him and move him further!

Too many negotiators from an Anglo-cultural background use compromise as their first choice when it should be their last, simply because any gains are easily quantifiable, and so it feels comfortable and fair. (No-one is going to be looking at the fringe benefits you may have missed if they were never part of the negotiation in the first place.)

Bargaining

Most books and films on negotiating concentrate their attention on bargaining. Most American business people will bargain with their customers and suppliers; the thrust of the US government's negotiating strategy has for many years been based on bargaining.

International and cultural divide

Some time ago the US government entered into a particularly complex negotiation with a South-East Asian government. It took place in Paris, but rather than hold sessions at their respective embassies, at the request of the French government the parties decided to lease chateaux in the suburbs of the city.

The Americans took their chateau for a fortnight, which they assumed would be long enough. Being typically positive and somewhat impatient, the Americans hoped to clinch a deal within a week or two. After a fortnight they had got nowhere and had to renew the lease. During negotiations, the South-East Asian party was extremely charming and attentive, but would not budge from their opening positions. The American party, anxious to make progress, began to give. And so it went on: the South-East Asians remained extremely charming and thankful for each concession made by the other party; and the Americans gave way but got nothing in return. Every fortnight, the Americans renewed the lease on their chateau.

After six weeks the American party was very frustrated. The South-East Asians smiled but refused to move. Naturally, the Americans' frustration was vented from time to time in front of the other party (who remained charming and in complete control). They would shout and bang the table. And after every tantrum they would feel guilty and they would give further.

The negotiation went on for 19 months, throughout which the Americans continued to give without getting anything in return. In the end they had nothing left to give, while the South-East Asians had still not budged. The US party's chief negotiator was later told that the South-East Asians had taken out a three-year lease on their chateau! (If the Americans had bothered to find out the duration of the lease, they might have gained some valuable insight into the way in which there opponents expected negotiations to progress.)

Research shows that once a person has given, they are more likely to give again. Once they are moving, they are more likely to continue moving, committed to the process and determined that the other party will respond sooner or later.

Rule one of bargaining: **Do not indicate that you are prepared to move quickly from your position**. While bargaining is about both parties moving, you will undermine the credibility of your own position if you move too soon. Should you do so the other party will dismiss your initial position as either extreme or without foundation. Once they have got you moving, you, rather than they, are most likely to make the next move. A common shortcoming of many negotiators is their predictability; do not get a reputation, for instance, of always taking a tough position but then consistently giving way on your demands. The opposition quickly pick up on your time-honoured tactics and will learn how to manipulate you.

Rule two of bargaining: **Move slowly, making the other party work for every concession they get**. There is an element of ritual about the negotiation process. If a negotiation is too quick, for example, then at least one party is likely to feel dissatisfied. If you buy or sell something, and you have not followed some of the basic steps of the ritual, you are likely to be unsure whether you have secured the best possible deal.

A riddle:
You pay 4100 for a car and you're happy.
I pay 4000 for the same car and I'm unhappy.
How come?

Imagine you are looking to buy a car and you see the model you want advertised at, say, 4500. You look the car over, it is what you want, and so you make an offer. You offer the seller 4000 for it, and immediately he accepts your offer. He doesn't try to pull a higher offer out of you; he doesn't even pause to consider your offer. He just about snatches your hand off. How do you feel? You quite naturally feel that you could have bought the car for much less had your starting price been lower.

Imagine now that the same car has been advertised, that you have made the same offer – 4000 – but this time the seller reacts differently. He says he won't accept your offer, but he is prepared to move. After a lengthy negotiation over the price, you and the seller eventually agree on 4100 for the car. How do you feel? Under these circumstances you feel you have worked for your concessions and have squeezed the best price out of the seller, even though you have ended up paying 100 more than in the first example.

Rule three of bargaining: **Avoid putting 'markers' down**. A marker is usually a figure – a price, a delivery period, a number of days' holiday – which is your ideal position in any negotiation. By putting a marker down you immediately put a ceiling on what you can achieve, and you could prevent the other party from moving further in your favour.

Returning to the example of the car, suppose you have agreed terms with the dealer for buying the new car and the question then arises of a trade-in price for your old car. The dealer will probably ask you: 'What figure do you have in mind?' He wants you to put a marker down. While it is not always easy, you should try to avoid giving the marker because you do not know what the dealer is willing to pay you for the car. If you give a marker and suggest you would accept, say, 3000, and that figure is within what the dealer was willing to pay, it will not be just accepted, but from then on the dealer will be under no pressure – the dealer can try to move your price downwards at no risk.

Avoid putting pressure on yourself and giving power to the other party.

In this situation, you would be the only party under pressure. Experienced negotiators take care not to put pressure on themselves, but to apply it to the other party. Some ideas for avoiding putting down markers are given in the section on openings in Chapter 10.

Rule four of bargaining: **Get a return for any concession you make**. In the case of the US negotiators it is clear that they continued to give in the hope that they would eventually draw a similar movement out of the South-East Asian party. They did not. With hindsight, it is easy to see how they fell into that trap. Many of us probably think it could not happen to us, but at home don't we sometimes find ourselves on the slippery concessions slope? You offer your children £3 to cut the lawn and they refuse, so you immediately up your offer to £5, thereby breaking one of the simplest rules of negotiation. It is an easy trap to fall into.

So stay in control and avoid the temptation to continue moving. People tend to accelerate when sliding down a slope, so consciously create rocks, trees, tussocks that you can grab onto to halt your slide, or from which you might even climb back up. For any concession you make, ensure you get something in return before you consider moving again. Bargaining is a process of *giving* and *taking*.

Avoid the slippery slope of granting one concession after another.

Because bargaining involves give and take over a range of issues, the question of value inevitably arises. A price increase in return for an improvement in quality and a swifter delivery: is it a good deal? You should always try to emphasize to the other party the full value and benefits of any concession you make. Conversely, you should play down and minimize the value and benefits of any concession they grant you.

Your success in bargaining will depend on winning greater value than you concede.

Threat/Coercion

Many leading European and American companies use coercion on their trading partners, in particular with their suppliers and their distributors, in the belief that by wielding their market muscle they will get what they ask for. Often they do. Yet what they ask for may not necessarily be the best deal going, and they may find themselves paying tomorrow for threats they make today.

Every single day big American and European corporations make bad deals by using their muscles more than their brains. My company was recently involved in a typical case involving a leading British food retail chain where its clumsy first approach and crude use of power eventually backfired. Obviously I cannot reveal the name, so we've called the company XYZ Supermarkets.

XYZ Supermarkets Inc. demands that Real Fruits, its tinned fruit supplier, drops its prices by precisely 15 per cent, *or else*; or else, presumably, it will take its big business elsewhere.

It cannot be denied that there are advantages to a dominant market position: it can help a buyer to get a better deal out of suppliers, but *only if it is used with great care*. Crude threats can be counter-productive. The XYZ Supermarkets buyer, by threatening to re-source, may secure the 15 per cent discount demanded. But ABC Stores, a leading competitor to XYZ Supermarkets, uses more subtle and more varied approaches in its negotiations with Real Fruits. It conducts its negotiations in a pleasant and respectful atmosphere. It uses approaches that support its position, including logical reasoning, perhaps about fruit market trends, and it uses bargaining techniques, perhaps in the form of offering to part-finance Real Fruits' future investment proposals.

As a result, ABC Stores secures an 18 per cent discount and slightly better payment terms for its tinned fruit supplies. And, should the tinned fruit market turn sour at some future date – if, for example, supply difficulty because of a poor harvest creates a severe product shortage and supermarkets are clamouring for supplies – which of its customers is Real Fruits likely to help first? Quite naturally, the directors of Real Fruits would probably enjoy telling XYZ Supermarkets that it will have to pay substantially more if it is going to receive anything at all.

Use brains before muscles.

In my seminars we have a short exercise that always creates substantial debate. We ask participants to draw a graph to illustrate the relationship between the *lowest* unit price that can be obtained for a particular item and the volume being purchased. Invariably participants draw a graph similar to Figure 7.2(a), which shows an inverse relationship between volume and price. This reflects what most people regard as a basic canon of commercial law: that the lower the quantity purchased, the higher the unit price.

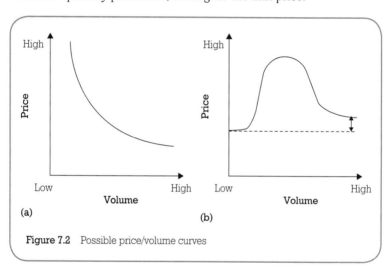

Figure 7.2 Possible price/volume curves

While this curve is valid in illustrating the relationship between *average* unit price and volume, our research shows that the graph in Figure 7.2(b) more accurately reflects the relationship for *lowest* unit price. This is because first class negotiators will often exploit particular commercial situations to obtain specially low prices for small volumes. Suppliers can be persuaded to make concessions for a small part of their sales which would be economically untenable for substantial quantities.

Going over the top

Another real-life example of threats backfiring happened with a food product a few years ago, just before a sudden world shortage of the commodity. A leading Mexican businessman, who was a major supplier at the time, met with one of the largest buyers in the UK who marketed a well-known brand and who also sold on as a wholesaler to other retailers.

The Mexican met the buyer and told him that, due to rising costs, he would have to increase the price of his supplies from, say, $2 to $3 a kilo. The buyer said no, quite emphatically, insisting that he could buy all the supplies he wanted elsewhere at $2 a kilo. He told the Mexican supplier that unless the latter held his price to $2 a kilo he would lose the business. Attempts by the supplier to shave his price back to $2.90 a kilo led nowhere: the buyer insisted that $2 was his limit and repeated his threat to re-source from another supplier. He could, he said, get all he wanted elsewhere at $2 a kilo.

The Mexican supplier then asked if the buyer was still wholesaling supplies, and if so, at what price his company was selling on to retailers. The buyer said his company was still in that market and that the mark-up was between 10 and 20 per cent. The Mexican asked if he could have an office and a telephone so he could ring his company. A little later he came back into the buyer's office with a written order which he handed to the buyer. It was an order to buy a large amount from the buyer's company at $2.40 a kilo ($2 plus 20 per cent)! The meeting ended abruptly with the buyer losing his temper and ordering the supplier out of his office.

The buyer then found that he couldn't buy elsewhere at $2 a kilo and that the market was moving quickly against him. He couldn't get adequate supplies to meet his company's needs and within three months supplies dried up entirely and a well-known brand disappeared for a short time. Several months after their meeting, the Mexican businessman released supplies back onto the market – at $11 a kilo!

Rule one of using coercion: **Before you threaten, think about the consequences**. Heavy-handed threats have a tendency to backfire on you, particularly when used against parties whose cooperation you may need at some point in the future. Even when closing one-off deals, such as buying an item or plant, remember that you may need to go back later for advice, spares, servicing, etc. Negotiators are ordinary people who do not easily forget being threatened. Given the opportunity they will get their own back. So do not go over the top.

  Rule two of using coercion: **Use 'mirrored' or emotional threats rather than crude ones**. The mirrored threat is where you paint a scenario for the other party and ask what they would do if they were in your shoes. That way you leave it to them to utter the threat and then you agree. This technique is unlikely to leave the other party feeling resentful towards you.

The emotional threat is different, but just as subtle. It is typified by the comment: 'Don't force me to look elsewhere for this product.' You are saying that you do not want to re-source to another supplier, but if you have to it will be the other party's fault.

Shoot yourself in the foot!

This 'kid-glove' approach was used to great effect by a purchasing manager within a UK engineering company. They had been instructed by the board of directors that for the third year running the company would be unable to accept any price increases from its suppliers. It was another zero–zero price freeze where they could not even balance one supplier's increase against a discount from another. There were to be no increases at all!

A castings supplier (let us call him AB Metals) telephoned to say he was looking for a 6 per cent price increase. He felt his case was reasonable as the increase would only cover his own cost increases for the coming year and for the previous two years. That was only 2 per cent a year, well below prevailing inflation.

The purchasing manager had been using AB Metals as a single source for castings for over two years, thereby getting a good price and enjoying low stock levels and just-in-time deliveries.

The purchasing manager told him there was *absolutely* no way they could accept any price increase this year. The supplier blew up and said he would stop deliveries the following month. The purchasing manager then went to work on him: 'This puts me in a terrible quandary. We went into partnership with you a couple of years ago in an effort to improve our quality and our stock control and to improve your planning horizon. We knew there were risks when we agreed the deal.

'Now I accept your view that a 6 per cent price rise over three years is perfectly reasonable. But you must understand that my board will not let me accept any price increases, full stop.

'I'll do what I can to help you in other ways – I'll try to increase volumes for you, I'll try to bring our payment dates forward. I'll try anything but I can't accept a price increase. What would you do in my shoes? I don't want to go elsewhere for supplies. How can you help me?'

While the purchasing manager retained their composure, the supplier became progressively more frustrated. The purchasing manager kept on asking him how he could help solve the problem. Then the flustered supplier shot himself and AB Metals in the foot. He said he knew of another castings supplier in Scotland which offered the same quality as

AB Metals, which had compatible tooling, and which was consistently undercutting his company on price. He didn't stop there. He then told them about another supplier based in a nearby city which had recently bought all AB Metals' redundant machinery. It was knocking one-third off AB Metals' prices!

If you want to flex your market muscle in a negotiation, remember that the veiled or suggested threat is always more potent and has minimal consequences. Furthermore, if threats are to be introduced, they should be used well into the negotiation. A threat used early on will put the other party in the wrong frame of mind either to move or to help you. Would you want to help someone who threatens you?

Logical Reasoning

In contrast to the hot-blooded southern Europeans who, stereotype claims, are prone to using emotion in negotiations, it is the, again stereotypically, cool, calculating Germans and Scandinavians who are the best exponents of logical reasoning in negotiation. When a good logical negotiator presents a case, say, for an increase in their prices, expect it to be backed by meticulous research, including a detailed breakdown of their costings.

This is where the buyer who asks the simple, reasonable question 'Why?' can land in trouble. For when the seller presents a reasoned, well-researched, detailed case backing such a position, the buyer can only resort to nitpicking. No-one likes people nitpicking their case, particularly when they can answer queries quickly and factually. This is not to say that a buyer should not seek further information or should not challenge the other party's case, but it must be done carefully and with sensitivity as to how the other party is reacting.

Imagine the buyer has asked for the reasons behind a price increase request and is given those logical reasons. Clearly the buyer will feel under pressure to accept the price increase, for to do otherwise would mean losing face through acting, apparently, irrationally. If the buyer then changes course and starts using emotive tactics like: 'Well anyway, we can't afford it', it is clearly a defensive move and the seller will be justified in going 'cold' on the negotiation.

Rule one of logical reasoning: **Be careful how you use the word 'why'**. Most people resent their logical position being picked over: they become frustrated if others quibble over minor details.

Question, but do not be pedantic.

Rule two of logical reasoning: **Get your logic in first**.

If you anticipate that a forthcoming negotiation will be following a strictly logical course – where you are trading facts for facts – it makes sense to get your logic in first. If you can explain in adequate detail why your company could not possibly carry a price increase this year and hope to remain in business, and you get this logic in before the other party is able to provide a perfectly reasoned case for such a price rise, you have taken the negotiating high ground. They then run the risk of being petty about your logic.

Rule three of logical reasoning: **Maintain the credibility of your logic**. If you are going to base your case on facts, make sure you have got them right and do not take the chance of assuming the other party will not check.

Caught out

Several years ago, my company was engaged in a consultancy capacity by a leading pharmaceutical company, which at the time was suffering a severe cash-flow problem. After other sources of working capital had been explored and ruled out, the company (let us call them AI Pharmaceuticals) decided its best option was to extend its trade payment terms. At the time, its average settlement period with its suppliers was 45 days. Its aim was to extend this to 70 days.

Most suppliers did not even notice when AI began paying its bills on a 70 day basis, and those that did accepted the extension. But a few initially refused to accept 70 day terms. We were brought into the negotiations with the reluctant suppliers and, within a couple of weeks, all but one company had agreed to the extension.

The very large supplier concerned (let us call it XYZ Chemicals) said it would allow AI Pharmaceuticals an extension to 50 days only. This, according to its sales director, was his company's average debt collection period. We saw this as a clear signal of a substantial concession: if his average debt clearance period was 50 days, then some customers were probably paying in 60 days! In view of this, we advised our client that we could probably negotiate 60 day terms or better.

The board at AI Pharmaceuticals was adamant, however, that every supplier would be paid on 70 day terms and no sooner, so we tried again. But we could not get XYZ Chemicals to move beyond 50 days and were told that XYZ would be stopping deliveries within 10 days.

Then we decided to check the credibility of the sales director's case. We tracked down the accounts of the particular division of XYZ concerned and established that its average debt collection period was not 50 days, but was in fact above the 70 days our client sought to achieve.

We rang the sales director of XYZ to tell him the good news: that AI's revised terms were better than what his company was typically achieving. This prompted an angry outburst in which he claimed that that the accounts bore little relation to reality, and that they were fabricated to satisfy the shareholders!

With the threat of delivery stoppage now looming, we wrote to the sales director, with a copy to his chairman, quoting what he had told us about the fabricated accounts. This was brinkmanship, but it worked. The chemical delivery arrived as usual the following week even though AI had already implemented the 70 day account policy, and deliveries continued thereafter unaffected. Two years later AI was still receiving 70 days' credit from XYZ, even though it had reverted to 50 day terms with its other suppliers.

Emotion

Emotion can be a very powerful approach in negotiation. After all, negotiators are not automatons. Indeed, if we examine many of the decisions we make, emotion plays a far larger part in them than we might care to admit. Like coercion, however, emotion has to be used carefully.

Take the security lock salesperson who used to sell his wares by playing on a very basic emotion: fear. Their patch was northern England, where they would tour all the new housing developments door to door. They would ring a doorbell, and when the home owner appeared they would be standing upright in the doorway with a large hammer raised above their head. Once the poor occupant had got over the shock, the salesperson would explain that with the greatest of ease they could at any time gain entry to the house by breaking a window and opening the flimsy locks the house builder had fitted. The emotional impact of the pitch was such that on some developments as many as 80 per cent of householders bought security locks from the salesperson. (Do note, however, that cold-calling with a sledgehammer may not be strictly legal in all jurisdictions!)

It is generally considered bad form to indulge in ethnic stereotyping, but many stereotypes (as opposed to blind prejudice) are based on observation. And it is observable that emotion, or more accurately the display of emotion, plays a large part in negotiations in areas such as southern Europe, which is hardly surprising as it fits with the personalities of many Italians, Spaniards, Greeks, etc. In Japan and other Far Eastern countries, by contrast, negotiators are often expert at controlling their own emotions while knowing how to trigger, to their advantage, emotional reactions in you. Indeed, in Japan, a display of emotion in a negotiation, unless this has been planned for maximum effect (which arguably counts as threat rather than emotion), may constitute loss of face. The Anglo-Saxon nations show, typically, yet another pattern. (I will discuss patterns and differences in different nations' typical negotiation styles in Chapter 12, but do bear in mind that despite the arguable validity of the stereotypes, you cannot predict an individual's approach to negotiation from his or her passport.)

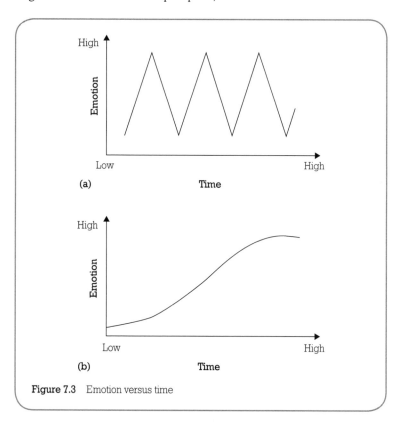

Figure 7.3   Emotion versus time

The two charts in Figure 7.3 show different temperaments. Which would you say typically reflected a southern European, and which a British temperament? To make a very general statement, one could say that a Spaniard or an Italian uses emotion constantly and will generally know how to bring it back under control. They flare up and cool down quickly. In contrast, it takes a great deal of provocation to upset the typical British person (the famed 'stiff upper lip') and when the British do react it is when they are reaching boiling point. The tendency of the British to bottle up their emotions until they reach extreme proportions is a much underestimated factor; some say it contributes to violence in British society, but undeniably in negotiations with other peoples it can contribute to a lack of trust. 'How can I have faith in someone when he is obviously trying to hide what he is really feeling?'

The field for emotional negotiation is almost boundless, but it does depend rather on what emotional tugs your opposite number is susceptible to. Salespeople may be able to suggest, 'If I don't get this order I'm finished', while this is slightly less credible for the buyer. But there are a lot of emotions you can call on; love, or at least liking: 'we've had a long relationship – you wouldn't want it to end in tears now'; pride: 'You've always been able to work something out for us – don't say you can't pull it off this time'; greed (although of course nothing approaching a bribe); fear (which is an emotion as well as a threat); even sloth: 'You will have a much easier life dealing with us if you can just agree to this one little point'; or jealousy, of another salesperson or of another company.

There is a lot to play with.

The first rule about emotion: Control your emotions; do not let them control you.

No matter how tough you want or need to be in a negotiation it pays to take a warm and courteous stance to begin with. Warm people and make them feel they want to help and be on your side.

The second rule about emotion: Use emotion early and be sincere.

A close friend for many years owned and managed a large holiday hotel. He noticed that most problems with visitors to the hotel occurred during the first few hours after checking in. I advised him to change his check-in procedure and increase staff handling arrivals, which were usually on a Saturday. Each visitor was to be given coffee/tea or a stronger drink at check-in, seated in the lounge and not stood at a desk! All were to be escorted to their rooms where they would be shown how everything worked and handed a complimentary box of chocolates.

Complaints virtually disappeared and repeat bookings increased. If you have ever been flattered by someone and it was done badly, leaving you with a negative reaction rather than a positive, then you will be fully aware of why it is important to use emotion with sincerity.

Remember

1. Compromise and bargaining demand two-way movement.
2. Emotion, logic and threat/coercion are potentially one-way movers.
3. Identify your preferred style and understand the rules for that approach. Then try and move your style/approach.

What Relationship?

8

Knowing that it is in our best mutual interests to succeed.

Successful business relationships rely on implicit trust and a determination to share in a common purpose.

The participants seek to understand each other's needs and, where there is a difference, negotiate to resolve the areas of conflict that prevent them from achieving the best result. The reconciliation of interests through negotiation calls for the practice of a high degree of interpersonal skill and a thorough understanding of the subject matter.

The best way to achieve a proper understanding lies in identifying and analysing the strategic areas of interest to each party. Managers should invest their resources in areas where tangible progress can be made towards attaining corporate and personal objectives. How does such an analysis fit into the selection process to determine the most appropriate relationship to match the business to be discussed? This question applies to any business relationship, even those within the company, but the simplest way to examine this question is to put it into a commercial context: a buying and selling one.

A buyer, for example, has to work out which supplies and services are critical to operational success, whereas a supplier needs to evaluate which customer accounts can best repay the investment in time and effort needed to retain and develop the business. Both need to decide what sort of business relationship will best achieve their objectives. The choices facing the buyer are illustrated in Figure 8.1 by a spectrum extending from the competitive, and strictly formal, arm's length setting, to one where vision and synergy are shared in a complementary partnership.

Purchasing, like other business functions, cannot be considered in isolation and decisions have to be made as to what relationship is necessary or appropriate. The type of relationship, whether it be arm's length, cooperative, collaborative or partnership, fundamentally affects the style and strategy of the negotiations within that deal. We are talking here about the relationship between

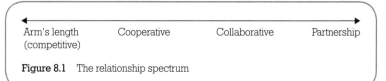

Arm's length   Cooperative   Collaborative   Partnership
(competitive)

Figure 8.1   The relationship spectrum

people and the organizations that they represent; not, usually, about the relationship appropriate to one specific deal.

A buyer may, conceivably, be negotiating the price of some simple commodity item that could, if necessary, be picked up on the high street. But the same vendor (possibly even the same salesperson) may be negotiating now or in the future around some much more strategic or critical supply. If the buyer in his or her ignorance gives the impression that the business relationship doesn't really matter much that could have major costs down the line. In addition, in many situations, suppliers are also significant customers!

Two techniques that are helpful in deciding the most appropriate relationship are:

■ supply positioning, as used by purchasing executives

■ supplier preferencing, as used by supplier account executives.

Each side, buyer and vendor, will, I hope, have used their own technique as a matter of course: the more clever part is to think yourself into the other party's shoes; to try to assess how you and your business stand in their scheme of things.

The relationship and application of these two techniques require explanation, providing as they do a method of channelling management effort into the most productive areas of the business likely to yield competitive advantage. The importance of these techniques cannot be understated. To quote Cox (2001): 'It is not whether a buyer or supplier possesses power over another that is the test of competence. Rather it is the ability by both sides to objectively understand the power circumstance that they are in that is the first requirement of competence.'

Supply Positioning

Supply positioning identifies, plots and segments purchases, relative to both their cost and the degree of risk they represent. (Supply risk is a book in itself, but it may include much more than the risk of interruption to supply, whether that is due to flood, fire, strike or a breakdown in commercial relations. It might include, for example, preferential access or the lack of it, to important new technologies that the supplier may develop.) The evaluation forms the basis for formulating a credible purchasing and negotiating strategy which embraces both the state of the supply market and the criticality, however that is assessed, of the item within the plot of a market segmented into four quadrants (Figure 8.2).

It can be time-consuming to list all the goods and services that are purchased for an organization and then plot them into the four quadrants as in Figure 8.2, but if the purchasing activity is to be lifted into a strategic role within the organization and contribute significantly to profit, cash flow and corporate development, then it is essential.

So how might your potential purchases map onto this matrix?

A major IT project, with bespoke software and a long-term commitment, would certainly meet the 'Strategic Critical' criteria.

Specialist fasteners, perhaps of an unusual grade of metal, or spare parts for machinery you still use, but which is no longer in production, might qualify for 'Strategic Security': not a lot of money is involved but you need to know you can put your hands on them.

Large orders of commodity-type materials, steel say, or standard fasteners (or in the service sector, basic cleaning and property services) might be areas where you can drive a hard bargain based on your buying power.

Low-value items that are crucial to the well-being of the business. Security of supply is more important than price. A hard negotiation would not be appropriate

Low value, low risk and low exposure. Unimportant items that are not essential to the business. You can put the supplier at some distance

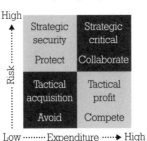

Key items that are both high cost and essential to the business. They are of the highest importance. Suppliers must be treated with care

Items not of crucial importance to the business but the high spend means that the buyer can play the market. Spot buying and hard negotiation are obvious tactics

Figure 8.2   Supply positioning

Pens, copier paper and water for the cooler probably fall in the 'Tactical Acquisition' box, *unless* it seems worth your while to upgrade the relationship. That can be a tough decision: often it means, for example, outsourcing the whole of office stationery supplies. That may give you a better unit cost, but does that outweigh the internal costs of managing a more demanding business relationship? It may, it may not. Where would you put the security outsourcing actioned by the excavator company mentioned in Chapter 4?

Supplier Preferencing

Supplier preferencing identifies, analyses and places the buyer's business in a segmented market made up to reflect the seller's vital interests (Figure 8.3). It enables the suppliers to evaluate the competitive position of their own firm in regard to other suppliers competing in the same market and to compare the attractiveness, or otherwise, of doing business when weighted against the relative value/cost equation. As with 'risk' in the supply positioning matrix, 'attractiveness' may cover more than the obvious criterion of profitability. There may be prestige and publicity issues: if you supply the gear lever knobs for Rolls-Royce, that may be business worth keeping at almost any cost even if it is small in volume. Similarly,

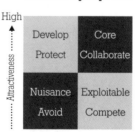

Customers who do not spend much but have enough attraction to make them worth pursuing. You would hope that your care and attention would prove rewarding

Customers of the highest quality who should be protected under any circumstances. You would not wish one of these to escape

Customers who spend little and are not at all attractive. Why are you doing business with them?

Customers who are not particularly attractive but who spend so much money that a great deal of profit and turnover can be created. You can negotiate hard and try to earn some money

The seller's perspective

High

Attractiveness

Develop	Core
Protect	Collaborate
Nuisance	Exploitable
Avoid	Compete

Low ····· Sales volume/margin ···▶ High

Figure 8.3 Supplier preferencing model

a supplier may value marginally profitable business because it allows him to share in his customer's research or technology, which he can then use to improve his offer to other, bigger volume or more lucrative customers. This is vital information to any supplier formulating a negotiating strategy, and the best insight possible into the supplier's thinking here is equally important for the buyer's strategy.

How might a supplier be seeing your business on this matrix?

Well, again, the big, long-term IT contract probably goes in their top right box (Core Collaborate). That is not quite a given though; if the contract looks as though it may be too big or demanding for the firm concerned, they may not be as interested as you might think.

Development projects, prototyping and so on may fall in the 'Develop Protect' box. Your supplier may not make much money out of you at the moment, but hopes that successful performance will lead to great things. (That does mean, though, that they might be going to offer you unrealistically low prices that cannot be sustained on a production order.)

Your bulk purchases of materials and services, where there is a lively competitive market, make up the 'Exploitable Compete' box (both sides will quite properly be trying to exploit and looking at competition).

You want penny-packet deliveries of a low-volume product, delivered to depots all over the country, and although it is almost a commodity product, you have insisted on a few little tweaks, which you are not prepared to pay for. The supplier ought to see this trade as 'Nuisance/Avoid'. If they do not, it may mean that they have some perversities in their sales/reward schemes, or that they do not know their own costs of doing business. That could make the company a golden opportunity for you, or it could be a serious danger signal, but beware: in this box could be something that was previously strategic and core to them but a change of priorities or policy has changed matters.

Matching the Parties

The best possible scenario is one where the buying and selling parties share a common belief that each can realize their respective goals through a contractual relationship that supports this aim.

Given that the analyses by the buyer (Positioning, Figure 8.2) and the supplier (Preferencing, Figure 8.3) are conducted entirely independently of each other, there is ample room for incorrect assumption and misunderstanding. Notice that although specifically similar, there is no reason why the matrices should not map onto each other (see Appendix 1). Two thoughts may provide a clue to clarifying the intentions of the parties:

- **Power**: What is the power balance both from a person-to-person perspective and from the respective business-to-business angles?

The parties need to understand where the sources of power lie and from where pressure can be anticipated. This is a factor likely to affect the negotiation and the ultimate choice of relationship.

- **Empathy**: Can we see and understand how and why the opposing party think and feel the way they do and what drives them?

The use of empathy calls for good listening skills and self-control. We need, however, to ensure that the fine line between empathy and sympathy is not crossed. Empathy involves being able to see why the other party is viewing you in a particular way (even if you believe or know that their analysis is wrong); sympathy would involve agreeing with the other party's analysis, in which case the game is probably up! If you believe that their view of you is wrong, what are you doing? How are you conditioning them to take a more helpful view of you?

The importance of finding out at the earliest possible stage in negotiation how much the other party wants the business cannot be overemphasized.

The answers to these and similar questions, which go to the heart of the relationship, need to be obtained at an early point in the contractual cycle. Care and attention have to be invested in a relationship to generate a genuine desire to reciprocate.

The Business-to-Business Relationship

Irrespective of outcomes derived through the impersonal application of positional analysis, such decisions require validation through skilled dialogue to discover real intentions. This is true not least because the counter-party may not be acting or thinking in what, to a machine, would seem to be the entirely rational manner: the prestige of supplying the Rolls-Royce gear knob surely exists, but is difficult to place on a positional analysis.

Any negotiation has, therefore, to take place on two interdependent levels if it is to succeed (Figure 8.4). Efforts will be concentrated in the personal dimension to detect and correct mismatches of business grouping or categorization. The aim is to achieve a better fit of the segments (as in the examples of buyer and

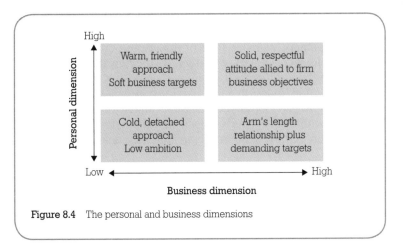

Figure 8.4   The personal and business dimensions

supplier analyses in Figures 8.2 and 8.3) towards an agreement of purpose which will ultimately underpin the relationship.

Collaboration

In the 1990s, in particular, much discussion centred on the ideal of partnership and phrases such as 'partnership sourcing' were the vogue, but this should never have been construed as a blanket endorsement of partnership or collaboration. Many business situations are resolved quite satisfactorily at other levels of relationship. A partnership is by no means the only way to resolve business relationships and may in some cases be inappropriate.

Collaborative research ventures, as witnessed in the aerospace and motor industries, show that possibilities can be jointly studied without the necessity for concluding a strategic long-term relationship, and even a long-term relationship on the research side need not commit to a long-term sourcing relationship. Neither contract size nor criticality is necessarily a criterion: if you are buying a new head office, that is expensive and critical but probably does not prompt you into a partnering agreement with your estate agent!

Beware of the wolf in sheep's clothing. I have encountered buyers in the manufacturing sector with minds set upon adversarial intent while professing a belief in the benefit of partnership, thus offering every prospect of a bumpy ride; indeed, such behaviour will fairly rapidly be seen as a sign of bad faith. Pilling and Zhang (1992) observed that 'power must be exercised judiciously'. The use of coercive power in inter-firm relationships has been shown to weaken their cooperative nature.

Figure 8.4 shows how types of relationship can be displayed, but avoids the obvious temptation of mapping these directly onto the superficially similar 4×4s of supply positioning and supplier preference. As stressed earlier, we are now talking about relationships between organizations as a whole, not about individual commodities and trades. In particular, the bottom left box 'Cold, detached approach; low ambition' may accurately reflect the mutual business relationship between organizations, but it is definitely not an instruction for how to approach an individual deal.

Horses for Courses

Figure 8.5 summarizes how the five styles of negotiation fit into the spectrum of strategic and tactical negotiations. There are few surprises; threat, for example, can be more usefully (and safely) employed if you are less worried about the long-term future of the relationship; logic and bargaining may be largely wasted if the discussion is purely about price in a commoditized market. Do note, though, that emotion is a winning style throughout. Also refer to Appendices 1 and 2 for more detail on a strategic context for negotiation and commercial relationships.

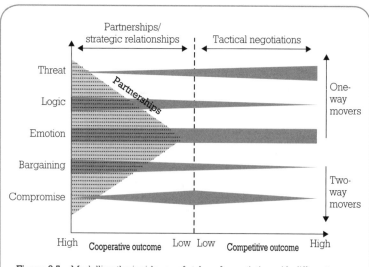

Figure 8.5　Modelling the incidence of styles of negotiation with different commercial relationships

Remember

1. Clearly establish the nature of the difference between parties before deciding on the kind of relationship that needs to be fostered. Will the time-frame matter?
2. Analyse the benefits and decide on the amount of effort needed to make the arrangement achieve what you want. How important is it to the business?
3. Think in terms of the other party. How attractive is the potential business to them? Do they need or want it? How does it fit into their portfolio? Clues to answers take effort to recognize. Signals in early negotiation will be detectable only if you empathize and share the concerns of the other party.
4. Study the balance of power between interests and the respective parties. Power may flow from a position or an appointment held, from the reputation of an organization or even from the latest development in the business picture. Expect leverage and conditioning from those used to exercising power, and be prepared to counter it.
5. Sales staff sell to customers but buyers deal with companies. Both deal with people as distinct from organizations, but it is a point for reflection on how the different roles are perceived.
6. Negotiations, once started, proceed on two levels:
   - the personal
   - the business (or task).

   Despite the excellence and accuracy of analytical methods any changes to achieve a best fit (congruence) will largely rely on the efficient functioning of the person-to-person level.
7. The choice of relationships (as examined in Figure 8.1) influences the style that the parties are likely to adopt, but any form of relationship is eventually going to be codified or represented by some sort of, probably written, contract. How much reliance is placed on the written word when such trust would have been better invested in securing commitment on the personal level?
8. Negotiation is a two-way street. From my understanding of its nature there needs to be a genuine desire to create a climate in which pledges of trust can be reciprocated. Shared warmth produces remarkable dividends once the parties are at ease and contributes to making the deal work.

9

Objectives, Preparation and Planning

> *'Negotiation research has found that parties often fail
> to realize the potential benefits in complex situations and that the
> failure is due to a lack of systematic planning'*
> *(Rognes, 1995).*

Without adequately defining your objectives, preparing your case and planning your strategy, your chances of achieving your objectives in a negotiation are minimal. It would not be overstating the case to say that the outcome of many negotiations depends entirely on how the parties prepare themselves and plan their strategies.

If one party has allowed just five minutes before a meeting to defining the desired outcome, planning how they will dictate the agenda, how they will open their case and how they will tackle some foreseeable tricky questions, they will always outperform someone who has given no prior consideration to the negotiation. The initial phase of a negotiation incorporates objective setting, preparation and planning; although these are different tasks there will very often be a degree of feedback.

Objectives are about defining in a succinct form the minimum criteria that will allow you to conclude that, if they are met, the negotiation has been at least relatively successful. (There is hardly ever such a thing as absolute success; there will always be some factor around which you could, perhaps, have achieved a better deal.)

Preparation is concerned with research: it includes researching your own precise requirements and latitude for movement, researching the market and the other party's strengths and weaknesses, and making some (educated) assumptions about the other party's *ideal* and *fall-back* position.

Planning is where you devise your strategy for the negotiation session(s). You imagine how you will open your case, how you will take the initiative by setting the agenda for the negotiation, how you will reduce the other party's expectations, and so on.

In this chapter I set out to improve your objective setting, preparation and planning by exploring, among other factors, the following:

- how to set your targets
- putting a cost on concessions
- perceptions and assumptions about strengths and weaknesses
- planning each stage of the negotiation
- how skilled negotiators prepare and plan
- research: sources of market intelligence.

Setting Objectives

All my experience and research with actual practitioners shows that generally the more we ask for the more we get, *but* we must not reveal the *actual* objective in the opening statement – study Appendix 4.

The fact is that reference points can influence the outcome of a negotiation.

(Kraus et al., 2006)

If we don't know where we're going, how will we know when we've arrived?

Your objectives should be a statement, as concise as possible, of what you need to have achieved to make a deal successful (or in some cases, possible).

Objectives are rarely single; usually there will be several overarching areas to be satisfied (for example, the appropriate product specification, but at an acceptable price, and with acceptable availability, and so on). For some negotiations there may be a hierarchy of objectives, especially if there is a suspicion that the 'perfect result' may be unattainable; or there may be alternatives; for example, 'We really want product X, at an acceptable cost; but if X is not available, we would accept product Y, but the maximum price we would accept then is commensurately lower', and so on.

It is almost blindingly obvious that the first objective is for a successful negotiation; almost, but not quite. In political negotiations it is not uncommon for negotiators to be set up to fail. The classic example is probably Austria's demands on Serbia before the First World War, which were deliberately pitched to make it impossible for Serbia to agree (actually, the Serbs agreed all but one clause, but the war still broke out). One can see the same thing in some industrial disputes where either labour or management, or both, seems determined to provoke a dispute, even while apparently negotiating under the auspices of neutral arbiters.

In commercial life, thankfully, this is rare, but it can happen. For example, many outsourced service contracts, particularly in the public sector, are struck for, say, five years, with a right of renewal for a further term. Political views may change or there may be a desire to bring work back in-house (or, equally, the contractor may have found the client to be impossible to work with). There may be no grounds on either side formally to break the contract, without incurring penalties, but it can be that negotiations on the extension of the contract are carried out less than entirely sincerely.

Normally, however, the prime objective is for the negotiation to succeed, however success is measured, and objectives and targets are a way of measuring that success.

The whole process of setting objectives for the negotiation may itself be the subject of (internal) negotiation. Your colleagues in finance, manufacturing, marketing, supply chain, technical/engineering and others may all have views, some of them contradictory, about what a successfully negotiated outcome would look like. Finance will want the lowest price (although they may not be able or willing to distinguish that from lowest lifetime cost); engineering or design may insist on a very tight specification, even to the point of specifying a proprietary brand. This should be challenged, to gain the negotiators the greatest possible freedom, but sometimes it is unavoidable: if your electronic product is sold on the basis that it has 'Intel inside', there is not much point in asking for leeway to negotiate a generic substitute.

Clear, succinct objectives are particularly important where the negotiation is to be carried out in teams. It is too easy for an enthusiastic negotiator to go chasing after a near-perfect solution to some aspect that is not, in the great scheme of things, of the first importance. Therefore, objectives need to be clear, concise and couched so that they limit alternatives only when absolutely essential.

At the same time, wherever possible, your objectives must be quantified. Only then can you accurately measure your performance. If your stated aim is 'To reduce the price you are paying', then have you been successful if the other party makes a token movement on price? Far better surely to have an aim 'To reduce the price by at least 8 per cent'. While performance in negotiation should not always be measured against a predetermined target (the target could have been based on assumptions that were wrong, or market conditions may be moving so rapidly that your research is out of date), nevertheless in most cases targets will provide a valuable yardstick.

We know of one organization with a highly skilled estimating department that sets targets for its buyers to achieve when negotiating with suppliers. By value engineering certain components, these estimators can accurately determine what the buyer should be paying (including a fair profit margin for the vendor). Interestingly, no account is taken of the conditions prevailing in the market: is it currently a buyer's or a seller's market? Yet currently most buyers are meeting the targets being set for them. Unfortunately, however, some of them stop negotiating when they reach their targets. A major computer manufacturer suffered a serious competitive disadvantage by being led entirely by engineering estimates. In one instance they were paying over $1 per component only to find within a year, following a change in approach, that they were paying less than 5 cents for the same item.

Being unaware of (like the buyers above who ignored the market conditions) or mistaken about some of the basic issues will affect your target setting, although sometimes to your benefit.

If only!

A relative was interested in buying a house which she had read was on the market for 157,950. When she had looked around it and found it was just what she wanted, she put in an offer of 145,000 to the seller, around 12,000 below what she believed was his asking price. Eventually she struck a deal at 153,000. Only later did she find out that she had misread the original selling price: it was 169,950 not 157,950, and had she known that at the time she would have felt embarrassed putting in the offer she did and probably paid more.

As I said earlier, setting objectives and targets will often constitute a negotiation in itself.

It may be that those charged with conducting the negotiation are not those with the responsibility for setting the overall objectives. They should be allowed to play a part in setting their own targets, at least being consulted by senior management, otherwise targets imposed on a negotiator can act as a demotivator. If targets are wholly unrealistic they will inevitably demotivate people. But even in cases where the targets are achievable, it is important for a senior manager to 'sell' the target to the negotiator so as to gain their commitment, and perhaps more vitally, so that they understand why a particular objective is important (and perhaps, why others may be less so).

When approaching target-setting, buyers or sellers often use their instincts, their own feel for what is achievable based on their experience of the market and of the other party. This can be dangerous. Instinct and some knowledge of current market conditions may leave a buyer, for example, poorly prepared for a negotiation: there is too much scope for subjectivity and bias. A buyer will be better able to set targets if he researches more factual information, including cost data.

Furthermore, where sufficient information is available, objectives should be set in terms of target ranges, reflecting a negotiator's ideal, realistic and fall-back positions. Setting a target range rather than a precise figure is good negotiating practice. As well as being easier and more realistic to prepare, it gives a negotiator flexibility. Golfers use target areas when they play their approach shot to the flag, finding it more realistic to aim at a target area than a precise point. Likewise when a negotiator tries to envisage what a good deal would be, it can be easier to imagine an area within which that deal may fall, rather than a precise point.

Here are some questions to ask yourself when preparing your target spectrum:

- What is the supplier's pricing policy?

- Can I find out the prices of their components?

- How keen are they to secure my business?

- How large would my order be to them?

- What conditions (price, etc.) have we achieved in the past?

- How strong/weak is our/their position?

- Have I conditioned their expectations, or have they conditioned mine?

But be wary of 'ideal' positions. As I have already suggested, new information can come to light in negotiation that can reveal whole new possibilities: if the negotiator is merely working in his or her 'ideal' comfort zone, such opportunities can be easily missed. Rather like the questions you ask in a negotiation, objectives and targets should be open rather than closed, to allow you to act on new information and in new or unanticipated situations.

To summarize, your negotiating objectives should therefore be:

- quantifiable

- high but attainable

- only bounded or limited where they need to be

- agreed by all concerned

- supported by cost analysis and other data wherever possible.

Set a target range, not necessarily a single figure, comprising ideal, realistic and fall-back positions, but with sufficient flexibility to allow the negotiator to adapt to new information.

Preparation and Intelligence Gathering

Setting objectives and targets for the negotiation cannot be done out of a blue sky. While there may be an 'ideal case' in the head of a senior manager, in reality the objectives and targets must be hauled back into the realms of reality when they are informed by all the information gleaned in preparation. (At the same time, the high-level view of what the ideal outcome would be will inform the direction of your preparatory work, and there will or should be an element of feedback.)

The information you are trying to gather together to support your negotiation will come from many sources, both internal and external.

Internally, one of the most important tasks is to put costs on any concessions that you may be likely to make. If you foresee that the negotiation will involve some bargaining, some give and take, you should arm yourself with a detailed breakdown of precisely how much particular concessions are going to cost you. You need to know how much it costs you to give up each inch of ground between your ideal position and your fall-back position. Doing hasty calculations during the negotiation not only appears unprofessional, it could be hazardous, as you could easily make a very costly mistake. One buyer I know returned from a tough, complex negotiation with his supplier, convinced he had reached agreement for the supplier to hold their average price increase that year to 1.6 per cent. When he sat down and worked it out again he realized he had conceded to a 16 per cent increase.

Always remember that it is not just in negotiation over unit price that you may be conceding cost. As an example, a vendor may offer a lower unit price if he can deliver, say, one 44-tonne truckload a week, rather than one 7.5-tonne load a day (the price reduction reflecting his lower transport costs). But if your warehouse has to put extra labour on to deal with such a big load, that may not be a good deal after all. Accepting a price rise in return for better credit terms is another common example. You need to have a firm picture of these cost and price issues at your fingertips throughout a negotiation.

Where possible, you should also try to cost the other party's likely concessions. This may identify a particular issue where any concession they make would be very valuable to you, but perhaps not too costly for them. This sort of background research can be extremely helpful.

When costing concessions, remember that you need not concede ground to the other party in tidy increments or round numbers, such as 1 per cent or 100 pounds, euros or dollars. When you move, you should move slowly and in small increments – see Chapter 7.

Perceptions and Assumptions about Strengths and Weaknesses

Your perceptions prior to the negotiation about the relative strengths and weaknesses of your position, and the position of the other party, will be based on several factors. Hopefully, among these factors will be some factual evidence of your relative market positions, although that information (even about your own organization) is rarely as complete or as current as you would like it to be. (If you have followed the techniques of supply positioning and supplier preferencing outlined in Chapter 8, you will already have done a lot of this.)

Other influences on your perceptions will be your own past experience, what you have read in specialist magazines, what you have heard from others in the business, and so on.

So your perceptions about both parties' relative positions are based on some reliable and some less reliable sources. Equally, the other party will have formed a perception of their strengths and weaknesses as against yours, and their perception, similarly, could be at variance with reality. Whether either party has got it right or not, the chances are your perceptions will be different from theirs.

If a buyer, for example, is faced with a company showing high profitability they could naturally assume that the supplier is in a strong position; similarly, they may regard a company achieving low profits to be in a weak position.

But profit itself is to some extent a matter of opinion. Profits can be raised or lowered according to stock valuation policy, capital and revenue expenditure policy, depreciation policy, and so on. Remember that companies achieving high profits face demands both from the tax authorities and from their own shareholders, so to improve their position companies will sometimes try to keep their declared profit down. Profit needs to be considered not as an absolute, but relative to the averages and norms in that particular industry or line of business.

At the preparation stage it can be helpful to have a colleague play devil's advocate by assuming the other party's position and thinking as the other party would. They could reveal weaknesses in your position or strengths in the other party's that had not occurred to you, but remember it is natural for us to focus on our weaknesses and the other party's strengths and we need to reverse this, focusing on our strengths and their weaknesses. One large international defence equipment supplier increased its fees from government contracts by 12 per cent by focusing on this method during its negotiation planning.

Given below are some pointers to relative market strength. In a buyer/seller negotiation, the buyer will be in a strong position when:

■ demand is not urgent and can be postponed

■ there are many potential suppliers and/or suppliers are very keen to obtain the business

■ the demand could be met by alternative or substitute materials/parts/services, etc.

■ there are 'make or buy' options available

■ the buyer has a good reputation in the market

■ the buyer is well informed about the supply market.

The supplier will be in a strong position when:

■ the demand is urgent

■ suppliers are indifferent about accepting the buyer's business

■ the supplier is in a monopoly or near-monopoly position

■ buyers want to deal with a particular supplier because of its good reputation

■ the supplier owns the necessary tools, jigs, fixtures, etc., or owns specialist machinery

■ the supplier is well briefed about the buyer's position.

We will always have to rely to a large extent on assumptions about the other party's position. When making an offer for a house advertised at 400,000 many of us would assume that the seller would be unlikely to accept anything below 360,000. We therefore would not offer any less. But there may be many circumstances under which a lower offer might be accepted: the seller's employers have asked for the move and offered to settle the difference between the asking price and what has to be accepted; maybe the seller is self-employed and needs urgent cash for the business. Divorce settlements, sadly, are a common factor. Or perhaps the house really is only worth

330,000. In a volatile market, you have to some extent to second-guess the vendor's view of future market conditions, which may not accord with your own.

Despite globalization, your perceptions, and those of your vendor, may be coloured by local and regional conditions, even if the product or service in question is traded internationally.

One buyer fell into the trap of assuming that the future will reflect the past. After several years of accepting large increases from his transport contractor, the buyer remarked to a colleague: 'I've done my calculations, and no way am I going to accept an increase of more than 106,000 for next year's contract.' He was used to getting his own way and he assumed the contractor would ask for more.

His colleague told him his assumption was dangerous and suggested he should probe what increase the contractor was looking for. During the early stages of the negotiation, and under questioning, the contractor said: 'Unless I get an increase of at least 70,000 then the contract is not worth having.' The negotiation proceeded and they settled on a 68,000 increase.

Any perceptions based on assumptions should be marked **RED** for danger.

Sources of Market Intelligence

The necessary market information on which your negotiating targets should in part be based can be gathered from a range of sources. The Internet has made intelligence-gathering a lot easier, and although you should not believe everything you read on the Web, just the same is true of old-fashioned printed media.

It should be remembered that you will continue to gather information during the early stages of the negotiation – during the testing phase where you test some of your assumptions – and also at the end of the negotiation when the other party, perhaps in a more relaxed mood, may give away information that you can use in future.

A couple of general points about intelligence-gathering are worth emphasizing.

Firstly, modern negotiations are often 'multiparty', although this may not be obvious. There may only be two people, or two teams, in the room, but the deal may affect and bind other parties. For example, if you are negotiating for the supply and maintenance of an IT system, or indeed for almost any capital project, you may only be negotiating with a lead contractor, but many other parties may be implicated: the maintenance may be outsourced to a third party, there may be a financial partner (on, for example, a leasing deal), there may be all sorts of subcontractors. It is as important to carry out intelligence work on these partners (who may well be doing most of the actual work) as it is to research the lead contractor. (Which parties are to be involved may itself be a topic for negotiation.)

Secondly, remember that in a negotiation you can legitimately consider and evaluate sources of information that would not be permissible in, say, a sealed tender bid. A tendering exercise has to have the same rules for all, and to break the rules, to sway the decision on the basis of gossip or innuendo, could leave you open to legal challenge.

In a negotiation, however (including post-tender negotiation), it is perfectly permissible to discuss and explore rumours, reports, perceptions and 'soft' information; indeed, it can be a very useful way of getting the counter-party to talk (and therefore to reveal their hand). If the trade press, say, is suggesting that a company is in trouble, or the new product you are interested in is not all it is rated to be, allowing your opposite number to explain why this is all wrong can be most revealing!

Here are some sources of market intelligence:

- internal company reports

- published journals and business and management magazines

- newspapers and association services

- informal contacts with suppliers – and the supplier personally

- visits to the supplier's premises

- published company reports and accounts

- websites

- agencies providing specialist services and published directories

- consultants and market-sector specialists

- contact with other buyers

- trade exhibitions, seminars, conferences, courses

- industry associations and subcommittees

- government departments and embassies

- enquiries, bids or tenders (and not just those relevant to this negotiation)

- information obtained during negotiations (the current one or previous ones)

- other colleagues in your company who have contacts with the supplier

- other contacts in the supplier's company (other than the salesperson)

- what you did last time!

Internal sources can be particularly valuable, and not just the obvious ones such as fellow buyers. You can learn a great deal from, for example, your goods-inward people, your accounts or credit control department (very often, remember, a vendor is also a customer), colleagues who have previously worked in that industry, or even for that company (although allowing a due measure of caution about any personal biases) and so on.

Planning Each Phase of the Negotiation

The middle phases of negotiation are opening, testing, moving, and agreeing or closing (Figure 9.1).

You need an overall plan for how the negotiation is going to proceed through these phases, and how each phase is going to progress. But a plan is only a plan: although you will use many of the tactics and methods described later in this book to keep the discussion as close as possible to your agenda, circumstances change. If dramatic new information appears, you must have the flexibility to roll with this and adapt the plan while still chasing the objectives. It is said that 'The plan is the first casualty of contact with the other party', but by good objective setting and preparation, and the use of the tactics I outline later, you should be able to keep most negotiations broadly on track.

An important consideration is that, as I have noted earlier, in many negotiations there are multiple objectives. To achieve them, each will go through the middle four stages of negotiation. You need to decide whether you are going to tackle these in order of priority. That may often seem the sensible thing, to get the big stuff sorted first, but sometimes it can be fruitful to tackle apparently minor issues first. For example, if the current business relationship is somewhat clouded – perhaps your own accounts department has not been paying its bills promptly – it may be useful to clear away this undergrowth, perhaps even spontaneously offer some small concessions, to improve the ground for the main engagement.

Another vital point is that you need to build pause-points into your plan. Remember that every element of the deal is provisional until the whole deal is put together. You do not want, for example, to chase the price negotiation all the way to a handshake before you have an understanding of the other elements in the negotiation and how they may affect price, cost and value.

A third consideration to bear in mind concerns the elements you are *not* negotiating about. There are almost certainly some points that are simply not negotiable (often around the technical specification or the delivery time). Precisely because these are not being negotiated over, it is highly likely that they are the most important features of all in any resulting deal or contract, so while you make it clear to the other party that these elements are not for negotiation, you do need to secure agreement or acceptance, and to plan the point at which you secure that agreement.

Housework

Here, I look at how to plan to ensure you get what you want out of each stage. One of the first issues to settle is the location of the negotiation. Many buyers prefer to negotiate on home ground. They expect the seller to come to them. Of course, sales staff are used to negotiating on buyers' premises and it does give them the advantage of being able to claim that certain information is not available to them. Such a tactic would be denied to them if negotiating on their own premises.

Negotiating on the seller's premises has its advantages for the buyer. It provides a chance to look at stock levels, to see capacity utilization, to examine quality control procedures, and so on. Sometimes, neutral ground may be best (and if you are negotiating your way out of a dispute, perhaps in industrial relations, this may be highly recommended).

So even before considering the middle four face-to-face phases of negotiation, there is some planning (and housework) to do, especially if you are hosting the meeting. Finding and booking a suitable room (do you need projection equipment? Probably not, but it may be worth enquiring whether your visitor intends or needs to use slides, PowerPoint, etc.), blocking phone calls, ordering refreshments, alerting and priming reception and organizing car parking.

Particularly important is clearing an appropriate length of time for the negotiation. If it is likely to be complex, or acrimonious, half an hour at the end of a Friday afternoon is probably not appropriate. Putting your opposite number under time pressure can be helpful, but you need to be sure that this does not put them under so much pressure that they cease to function as negotiators (or just walk away), and also that you are not putting yourself under undue pressure. If you are expecting the negotiation to take more than one round of meetings you should plan accordingly (and probably advise your opposite number).

The notes below assume that the negotiation is 'one on one'. As I have noted, very often teams are involved, and this makes planning (and rehearsing the plan) even more vital. Everyone involved must understand what the plan is, how they contribute and, just as importantly, where they are expected to back off or keep quiet. You will probably also want to designate someone, if you are not doing this yourself, to take notes and to keep a running score of the various points of provisional agreement reached.

The following suggestions are designed to fit each phase of the negotiation. In your mind's eye you have to envisage the whole negotiation right through to completion. What is likely to happen at each phase? Tips on how to execute some of the tactics suggested here are given later in this book. The issues are viewed here from a purchasing perspective, but the principles apply to any negotiation.

Face to Face: Issues to Deal with During Planning

1. Opening Phase

1 Decide on the type of opening and opening statements to be used.

2 Identify common-ground issues that can usefully be mentioned to ensure that the negotiators present at least start together (e.g. agree purpose, recap on previous discussions, common problems/opportunities).

3 Decide how to phrase the requirement for the goods or services needed, saying enough to start the discussion but not to reveal your total hand. Write a point-by-point summary to refer to.

4 Plan credible and realistic comments about your own needs, and credible but 'diminishing' comments about the seller's claim or position.

5 Decide tactics for gaining and keeping control.

2. Testing Phase

1 Predict the supplier's questions and arguments and decide how they will be answered or defused.

2 Phrase open questions to test your own assumptions and to encourage a free flow of information from the supplier.

3 Anticipate the reasoning that the supplier will use to support his position and gather facts and arguments to undermine it.

4 Plan how to find out the supplier's 'shopping list' and how to avoid revealing your own.

5 Anticipate which persuasion mechanisms will be used by the supplier and prepare to match them and be ready to use appropriate persuasion methods to move the other party towards you.

3. Moving Phase

1 Work out the cost of concessions for each negotiation variable, and estimate what the costs to the supplier might be.

2 Decide the 'concession increments'.

3 Decide what concession trade-offs will be cheap to you but will be valued by the supplier.

4 Assess what personal or corporate needs the supplier has which the buyer, or the deal, may be able to satisfy.

5 Plan how the supplier can concede without losing face.

6 Make plans for overcoming deadlock … and adjournments.

7 Plan responses to any 'dirty tricks' that may be played.

4. Agreeing Phase

1 Prepare your closing tactics and other actions that will help to establish common ground agreement.

2 Decide how to obtain the supplier's confirmation of the points agreed and for the buyer to retain control of the summarizing/recording process.

3 Prepare proposals for steps to keep talking if agreement has not been reached.

4 Assess what information the supplier may reveal during post-agreement relaxation, which he is not prepared to divulge during the earlier discussions.

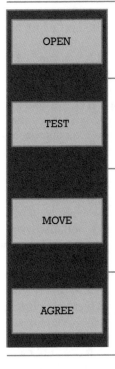

Objective setting preparation and planning	■ Fully understand the requirement ■ Research the market ■ Research the other parties ■ Ideal, realistic and fall-back positions ■ Supply positioning/supplier preferencing ■ Location selection ■ Plan the middle phases ■ State assumptions ■ Consider and value variables
OPEN	■ Warm and tough approach ■ Create rapport ■ Link openings to outcomes ■ Condition other party's expectations ■ Take control sensitively but firmly
TEST	■ Test own assumptions ■ Test other's position ■ Obtain information 　– by asking questions 　– by listening 　– by looking
MOVE	■ E, L, B, T, C (negotiating styles) ■ Listen for verbal and look for non-verbal signals ■ Control concessions – trade them and know their cost ■ Make creative proposals – don't expect the other party to always make the suggestions
AGREE	■ To reach a joint workable agreement ■ Record what has been agreed ■ Summarize ■ Agree the next steps ■ Condition for the next time
Review	■ Compare result with objectives ■ Extent of plan achieved ■ What could I have done better? ■ How did the team perform? ■ What persuasion methods were used/worked? ■ How did the other party perform?

Face to face

Figure 9.1　Phases of the negotiation: what's going on?

How Skilled Researchers Prepare and Plan

Research into the ways in which negotiators prepare and plan has found that there is very little difference between 'effective' and 'average' negotiators, in terms of the amount of time they allocate to planning. But there is a significant difference in the way the two groups use their time.

For instance, I have found that effective negotiators envisage a far wider range of potential variables, openings and outcomes than the average negotiators; in fact, nearly twice as many. Effective negotiators also spend more time considering areas of common interest between themselves and the other party over which bridges could be built to reach agreement.

Another key difference that I have observed is that average negotiators anticipate discussing item A then item B, followed by item C and item D. If the business is in any other order, they are thrown off balance. Effective negotiators, however, are able to discuss the agenda items in any order. They do not rely on the other party following their agenda, but are flexible in their approach.

Consider your Variables

Throughout the negotiation you will be juggling a larger or smaller set of variables – all the facets of a potential deal that could be modified in one way or another to give either or both parties a gain.

Although the list is potentially endless, Figure 9.2 shows some of the features potentially under discussion for a supply of goods. Many supply contracts nowadays also have significant service elements, whether these be in maintenance, after-sales, or in supply chain fields such as vendor-managed inventory; and there are pure service contracts which will have their own set of potential variables.

Bear in mind that, as already stated, just because some or many of these are 'non-negotiable' in a particular deal, it does not mean that they do not have to be discussed and agreed explicitly. Equally, many of these can be further subdivided, 'salami-sliced', if that seems appropriate to the negotiation.

Contractual	Pricing
Buy back	Volume discounts
Consequential aspects	Rebates
Duration	Breakdown/analysis
Liquidated damages	Stability
Terms and conditions	Deferral of increase
Third party liability	Payment terms
Authorship of contract	Currency
Health and safety	Installation costs
Insurance	Delivery costs
Inventory	**Relationship**
Buffer stocks	Confidentiality
Consignment stocks	Exclusivity
Collection of surplus	Sole supplier
Spares	Risk sharing
Unit of issue	Flexibility to changes
	'Guinea pig' to customer
Product	Supply chain
Assistance with trials	Audit rights
Commissioning	
Customization	**Specification**
Free samples	Manuals/drawings
Developments	Plans/critical path
Product endorsement	Training
	Performance guarantees
Production	Materials for testing
Quality/reliability	Tool kits
Supply security	Packaging
Flexibility	Progress reports
Lead time	Emergency response
Just in time	Translations

Figure 9.2   Potential variables

Remember

1. The most thoroughly prepared negotiator will be confronted with unforeseen events (Kraus et al., 2006).
2. Set clear objectives.
3. The more time spent in preparation and planning the better.
4. A negotiation goes through distinct phases.
5. Keep searching for variables.
6. Focus on your strengths and their weaknesses rather than your weaknesses and their strengths.
7. Successful negotiators focus on 'how' they are going to negotiate rather than just 'what' they are going to negotiate about.

10

From the Opening to the End of the Road

It is very likely that the opening will predetermine the basket of outcomes available to conclude an agreement. So right from the start do not create an unacceptable level of dependence by the deal that allows the other party to act opportunistically.

Controlling and Leading

An expert negotiator will take control of a negotiation. Assuming control will help to ensure that the right agenda is followed and that the environment is created whereby you can make your points effectively and stay clearly focused on your objective.

Taking control results from good preparation. You should have a clear route map of the negotiation: from the opening to the end. To help achieve this have your questions prepared and use them wisely. It is questioning rather than making statements that provides control. Questions force the other party to listen and concentrate ready to respond. Unbroken statements allow them to switch off, relax and even ignore you. But be careful you know the 'right' question and when to ask it. See Chapter 7 for how not to use 'Why?'

Use behaviour labelling and preface your comments or actions with a statement that tells the other party to be ready for what is about to happen. For example, if you preface your question with, 'Let me ask you a question …', you are in fact saying to the other side: 'I want you to listen. Please be quiet!' This is a most effective way to ask questions and ensures that they carry maximum weight.

This technique also allows you to interrupt the other side when they are talking, with words like: 'I wonder if I could interrupt you a moment. I'd like to ask a question …' If you combine this with stretching out your hand in an assertive way you will nearly always find the space that you are seeking.

At the beginning of the negotiation, towards the end of the social phase, you should make the first move with comments that suggest that it is time to start and that you would also like to discuss certain issues first: introduce the agenda. The other party may wish for the same so negotiating the running order may be the first important step of the meeting.

If you progress with the assumption that your agenda is the obvious way forward you may find that the other side goes along with this.

In planning your agenda you may not have put the most important (from your point of view) objectives first. Depending on the circumstance it may seem important to resolve, as far as you can, key issues such as price first, whereas in other negotiations it may be more appropriate to spend time clearing up minor and peripheral issues first. Either way, bear in mind that cost (as opposed to mere piece price) cannot really be resolved until all the other negotiable variables have been resolved: if you have 'shaken hands' on a firm price early, how could, and why should your opposite number offer you any concessions of value?

Ensure that you maintain control of the timespan of the negotiation. If the meeting is to last one hour then do not leave issues that are vital to you until it is too late to discuss them fully – a common error of the unskilled.

This is even more important when you visit another office and do not have total control over the environment. Do not allow the other negotiator to dictate terms merely because you are playing away. This is also important when negotiating abroad. Your journey times must be clear in your mind and you should not allow yourself to be manipulated. If negotiating overseas, be wary of the overnight flight followed by a big welcoming banquet. You may not be at your best at 8 am local time the next morning!

At any stage of a negotiation you always have the option to ask for a recess. This can be a genuine visit to the toilet, a need to clarify or make a calculation, or a tactical ploy to disrupt the opposition.

Be aware of these breaks and if you have coffee booked for a given time then do not allow the coffee to arrive just as you are making your most important point. At the same time you should know that whenever the negotiation gets tough it is a legitimate response to ask for some time out to reconsider some numbers, call back to base or consult colleagues. As mentioned in Chapter 9, I was once asked to advise a leading car manufacturer who had accepted a 16 per cent price increase on a range of components believing, initially, it had only paid 1.6 per cent; believe it or not important calculations had been made without a recess and not by an inexperienced or junior person!

Glass negotiation

For many years in training programmes I have run an exercise that involves selling a million wine glasses for 10 cents each or $100,000 in total for the order. During the negotiation the buying team usually ask for a discount, for example down to 8 cents each. I take the sales role and usually respond after some time by saying I will give them a rebate of $2000. Now this doesn't equate to a price of 8 cents. Eight cents would equal $20,000 off, but at this time, because there are a lot of figures flying around, many a buying team over the years has equated my offer of $2000 to meeting their 8 cents discounted price, thus making a major miscalculation. You would be surprised how many well-known business people have made this mistake.

Manage the environment to your maximum personal benefit. This is not the same as making your opposite feel uncomfortable. You want this person's best, not his or her worst.

Remember

1. Have a list of questions ready and work through them.
2. Make it clear that you wish the meeting run to your agenda.
3. Learn and practise how to interrupt politely.
4. Preface questions and interruptions with a behaviour label.
5. Keep track of the time-frame of the negotiation.
6. Use breaks and recesses to maximum effect.
7. Put your important points high on the agenda – do not leave too little time for them.
8. Keep your objectives in clear sight – the importance of this to success cannot be overstated.
9. Check the figures: rebates, discounts, etc.

Above all, do not reveal your objective(s) and do not put a marker down (see Chapter 7 and Appendix 4). Focus on your strengths and their weaknesses. Do not be intimidated by power; rather, focus on the limitations of their power.

Mind your Language

You cannot become an expert negotiator without an understanding of the power that words and language can have within a negotiation.

Expert negotiators have the ability to choose and manipulate words to an extent that would surprise most ordinary negotiators.

There is a need to stress the importance of the effect that terms and conditions can have on the outcome of a negotiation. Knowing as we do that the price is not the cost, the loading of words within the terms and conditions can prove crucial.

A good example lies within the realm of payment terms. Think for a moment of the many ways in which a buyer can pay for product or service:

■ cash on delivery

■ net monthly

■ bank transfer

■ pro forma invoice

■ direct debit

■ choice of currency

■ extended terms

■ invoice by electronic mail

■ credit card (and remember the charges levied by the card companies on the vendor, which will be passed on, you can be sure).

These are just a few. They prove that a negotiation cannot be complete until every last word is agreed and signed off. 'We can give you favourable payment terms' can mean many different things to many different people.

Expert negotiators routinely choose their words with utmost care. They have the ability to think in real time, to hear what is said and react immediately with their own careful choice of words.

Most expert negotiators hate having to say 'no' and will avoid anything that seems to close the door on a specific issue. If you work on the principle that anything is negotiable then you will be reluctant to rule something out. Therefore expert negotiators avoid negative words at all costs. Salespeople, especially, will not wish to walk away from a potential sale. If the offer is not what you want then build, develop, encourage, but most often avoid outright rejection.

Here is a list of phrases that are often used to avoid saying 'no', and the real meaning that should be attributed to them. Key 'signal' words are in italics.

Statement	Meaning
It would be *almost* impossible to move on that price	There's more left if you care to ask for it. 'Almost' is a signal
As things stand it would be impossible to change our pricing	We are flexible and can change if you push us hard enough
We do not *normally* offer discounts	We always give discounts to special customers
I'd find it hard to give you any more	There's more left
There are *only crumbs* left in the cupboard	There's more to give (what size crumbs?)
It's not our *usual policy* to give discounts	I can make an exception for you

Some of these quotations are theatrical but still provide a strong message. Listen to what *exactly* is being said and choose your reply carefully.

'This is my final offer' is one statement that has to be taken most seriously. By definition there can be only one final offer. Once you have uttered these words, therefore, you should be very certain that you mean them.

If you move on a 'final offer' your credibility is torn to shreds. Nothing you can say subsequently can have any value if the other party knows that there are several versions of 'final offer'. If you are negotiating with a person who moves from any form of final position be assured that this person is someone whose words cannot be taken seriously.

From a buying perspective very rarely ask for anybody's final offer. If they give it and it is not enough, what can you do? Also, if you do have to issue a 'final offer' do not dilute the power of it by adding a reason or an additional statement (see Chapter 13, Scenario 11).

It pays to tape-record your own voice to see if there are any individual words or phrases that you repeat continuously or that when used may cause offence.

Too many 'y'knows' or 'likes' at the end of sentences can readily stop people wishing to listen to you. Calling someone 'my good man' or 'darling', for example, is likely to cause offence and be wholly counter-productive. In some instances legal ramifications may even ensue.

Telling somebody that this is the 'deal of the century' is not likely to endear either you or the deal to them. Make your language appropriate both professionally and socially.

Lastly, one should avoid clichés, jargon, management speak and acronyms. These often create antagonism and such phrases as 'touching base with customers' and 'running ideas up the flag pole to see who salutes them' make most people shudder with embarrassment.

Remember

1. Check every written word carefully, especially when the document has legal consequences.
2. Listen for the real meaning behind the words.
3. Try to talk and think at the same time.
4. Do not use words like 'final' unless you really mean them.
5. Do not use offensive language and avoid clichés.

Non-Verbal Communication

The nature of communication has often been examined by experts and the following statistics, mentioned also in Chapter 2, are commonly quoted concerning the different ways in which communication takes place:

- 55 per cent non-verbal

- 38 per cent tone of voice

- 7 per cent words.

These figures reveal that non-verbal signals are very important (Mehrabian, 1981).

Many good books have been written on the subject of body language (Pease, 1997) and what seems to be particularly important is the manner in which body language matches your words and tone of voice. When you are able to combine all three elements, the point you wish to make is the more greatly emphasized and the other party is left in no doubt about your intentions.

A good example is when you wish to stress the importance of a subject. The choice of strong words such as 'This is nowhere near what I'm looking for' combines with a powerful tone of voice and gestures to add even more weight. Good eye contact and the use of the hands to push home the point will tell the other party that you mean business without antagonizing them. However, seeming to stare at people can be intimidating, and sometimes suggests that you have something to hide.

You must ensure at all times that your tone, words and body language are congruent. They must add value to your ideas and not detract from your argument. There is little point in making a good point if your voice is quiet and you are sitting with arms and legs crossed looking thoroughly defensive. You must ensure that the words 'fit the music'.

Some elements of non-verbal communication are particularly important in negotiating. The following points are those that every expert negotiator should know and use.

Eye contact. The importance of eye contact can never be underestimated. It is one of the most important means by which humans communicate. You must avoid looking away at a key moment. When the words are loaded with emphasis, eye contact will give them even more impact.

As children we are taught not to stare, and some people find too much eye contact threatening.

Salespeople are often advised not to wear tinted lenses if they wear spectacles. The customers need to see their eyes. Would you buy double glazing from a salesperson wearing sunglasses?

Body position. Always try to sit up to a table with your arms on the table. If you place your hands in your lap it will stop you using your hands to emphasize a point and will also prevent you from taking notes.

Smile and nod. This is a classic listening posture. It will encourage the other party to continue talking and will make you seem engaged in the business. This is particularly important when you are negotiating in a team and one of your colleagues is talking.

Be a mirror. A very subtle technique which helps to create rapport with the other side is to try to mirror their gestures and also to listen to their words. Check for any particular word that seems a favourite which you can then return to them at a key moment.

Be careful not to cause offence. If mirroring is done well it helps to cement a bond of trust across the table from which good deals will flow but be wary of subconsciously mirroring accents, dialects, or even hand and facial expressions. It is human nature for us to adapt our behaviour towards that of people we are trying to influence or impress, but it can very easily be mistaken for sarcasm or mockery. Do not pretend to be what you are not: you will be found out, and it may cause offence.

Remember

1. Make sure that your tone of voice fits the words and that your words are backed up by assertive gestures.
2. Maintain good eye contact, have a positive posture and be a friendly audience.

Try to reflect back to the other party the tone, words and gestures they are using to you. Make them feel at ease when dealing with you.

When Do We Start?

If you are thinking about when to start a negotiation it may already be too late. It may have started much earlier than you thought (refer to Chapter 4). Commercial negotiations start even before the first formal meeting: at an informal encounter, when a party has sent a speculative letter ('I understand you are interested in X – how can we get onto the bidding list?'), a telephone or, these days, an email query. It is never too early to begin in terms of conditioning the other party, shaping their expectations or creating a powerful first impression. And the end of one negotiation could be the beginning of the next one.

At the personal level the power of the first impression is well understood. 'Love at first sight' certainly makes the negotiation go more easily! Even before then the quality of the notepaper, advertising or just the efficiency of the administration creates the right sort of impression.

Conditioning (see also Chapter 4)

A powerful impression shapes expectations. It should be your desire right from the outset to condition the other party that they are dealing with a serious professional and their expectations should be set accordingly. If you get it wrong then their aspirations may rise before you have even sat down at the table.

■ This applies to the way that you dress, the car that you drive and the demeanour that you bring to the table. All of these should be part of your plan. Ensure that you use every means to create a winning impression, but you have to be sensitive to the scenario, while being true to your and your company's essential ethos. For example, a business suit, a well-maintained (not necessarily top of the line) car and a fairly formal approach may be appropriate if you are negotiating with a merchant bank. By contrast, a more relaxed dress style, arriving on public transport and less formal behaviour could be more effective if you are negotiating with a more 'youthful' start-up company. But if this is really alien to your nature, or to the style of your company, don't do it: people of all types and backgrounds are sensitive to the 'fraud' or the person who is just trying too hard.

Beyond this, here are some essentials that will help you to condition the other party in a favourable way. If you fall down on these you may still 'condition', but in the sense of conditioning against, rather than for, your interests.

- Ensure that your paperwork is faultless.

- Make your telephone contacts (and emails, texts, etc.) professional.

- Sow some seeds of ideas to shape expectations.

- Ensure that the negotiation room is well prepared.

- Prime your reception desk to expect and welcome your guest.

- If you are meeting at a neutral venue of your choosing (for example a hotel equidistant between you), as far as possible ensure that the staff there know and provide your requirements in the way that your own staff would.

- Do not keep anyone waiting unduly (and if there are unavoidable delays ensure that these are explained).

You want the other party to come into the room with low business aspirations and you should say or do nothing to jeopardize this. But conversely, you also want them to feel respected and valued as individuals. It is that 'warm but tough' thing again (see Chapter 4).

Some Preliminary Digging

Most preparation hinges on what you are going to do when you get to the meeting. Expert negotiators have already dug the ground. Plan to send some preliminary documentation, some information material or anything that may help to shape the perceptions or expectations of the other party in a direction favourable to you *before* the meeting.

Negotiations may spring from very tentative first contacts ('Could I come and discuss how we might be able to help you?') or from a very defined framework, for example, in post-tender negotiation where the other party has won the contract on price or whatever, and you are now negotiating over the modalities of delivery; and from every position in between.

If you are starting from a tentative (on either side) position, you want to have prepared the way with ample, but non-committal, information: freely offer company reports or anything else already in the public domain, but be reticent about volunteering more confidential information. The more specific the negotiating start point is, the more appropriate it may be to furnish hard data, forward plans, etc., but always filtered by the thought, 'How is this going to affect their view of my needs and expectations, and how will this information affect their expectations?'

There is also the rare, but plausible, case where you may be 'negotiating about negotiation'. For example, you may be approached by someone with a genuinely innovative product or service and they feel you would be the ideal launch customer, but for obvious reasons do not want you to take the idea out to open tender. So there may be preliminary negotiation, and even legal agreement, on how future discussions are to be handled.

Remember

1. It is never too early to start the negotiation.
2. Be aware of the power of first impression.
3. Manage all aspects of your behaviour and keep them positive.
4. Do your best to reduce the aspirations of the other party.
5. Keep emphasizing one or two key points, and/or feed them appropriate information and background, before the meeting to sow some seeds in their minds.

The Opening Round

When and Where?

It is now time to meet the other party. Of course you must, yourself, decide on where and when, and that will depend to some extent not only on the urgency of your requirement, but also on the level of preconditioning or softening up that you have felt it appropriate to do. (You probably want to display genuine interest, otherwise what's the point of a meeting at all? But you do need to allow reasonable time for the other party to absorb such information and briefing as you have seen fit to give them.)

Make sure that you place the meeting at the location best suited to yourself and least suited to the other party (although not to the point where the other party feels actively dissuaded). If you are a buyer, for example, you should be aware that salespeople routinely work away from home: your office is their home. Why not visit them? Remember, it is much easier to leave when you are in the other party's office; depending on how you think the negotiation is likely to go, your own base may not be best suited. And in complex negotiations, for example where a subcontractor is likely to be doing most of the physical work, even though your contract may be with the main contractor, meeting at the 'subbie's' place may make sense.

If you do have the meeting at your office make sure that the room adds to the impression. If you are based in an open-plan office borrow a room. Manage the location to provide the impression you require.

Consider also the timing. Very few sellers want to talk on a Friday afternoon. How many buyers would visit a supplier first thing Monday morning?

Be aware of your own body clock. If you are a lark have an early meeting and use your morning energy. If you are an owl do not be bleary eyed at an early meeting when you could be motoring in the afternoon. If people (on your side or theirs) are flying in from overseas, jetlag is a factor to be considered. Having your team fresh, and theirs jaded, can be an advantage, but only up to a point. If they are really too tired to function effectively, the negotiation outcome may be suboptimal, to say the least.

Face to Face

Now it is time to meet. Remembering what we know about first impressions we know how vital this stage is. You will never get another chance to manage your relationship with other people as much as you can during this first meeting.

Who am I?

Now that you have met it is time to acknowledge them personally. Who is he or she? What is their role in the company? Did he or she have a good journey? Would they like some refreshment?

When faced with a team of negotiators you should try to discover if one of the group is the decision maker. Once you have this knowledge you can direct your arguments accordingly. The obvious counter-ploy is to ensure that you do not reveal this to the other party. You can call yourself the 'project team' with joint responsibility.

Ask yourself, 'Why be hated when you can be liked?' This is the best way to start: slowly and with proper observation of the social niceties expected within the culture, which acknowledges their visit as valued guests (or vice versa), makes them feel warm towards you and starts the questioning process, whereby you can start checking your assumptions and validating your research.

Finding out who everybody is, and what responsibility or authority they carry, is rarely as simple as reading their business card. 'Executive Vice President' can cover anything from office boy to billionaire. In addition, a lot of executives seem these days to have alternative job titles, depending on who they are talking to and in what context. (For example, a person may have 'Managing Director' on their card as MD of a subsidiary. That may or may not mean that they have any presence on the main board of the holding company; and the holding company may or may not be a factor. If you are simply trading, perhaps it is not; if your negotiation is going to suggest that they commit some capital expenditure to meet your requirements, then perhaps this distinction does matter!)

The Power to Negotiate

One of your first tasks is to check that the person or team opposite has the power to negotiate and the authority to take decisions. You could be putting yourself to a great deal of inconvenience and time wasting if the other side has to report back and lacks the required authority to make a decision on the spot. You could give a lot away and get nothing in return. If you are not sure of someone's status, phone their switchboard, or get someone else to phone, and explore. (Your receptionist, obviously, is not the sort to give away sensitive details, but theirs might be!)

Who's Normal Around Here?

When questioned, most people from whatever walk of life will admit to being pretty 'normal'. That means a regular way of dressing, talking, behaving, having normal social, moral and political views, etc.

People feel most at home when they are dealing with others who are 'normal' like them. This creates a state of rapport and allows people to relax and feel that they are dealing with someone who they can trust. This is why people join clubs and societies and wear badges that identify them as 'normal' to fellow club mates.

People prefer to deal with people like themselves. If you build empathy and rapport they will see you as a 'like spirit'. The more the other parties see themselves when they look at you the easier they will find it to do business. An expert negotiator is, therefore, a social chameleon changing to suit each individual with whom they have to deal.

When this technique is used badly it looks artificial and manipulative, but when used subtly the usual feeling is one of trust and understanding. As noted earlier, forcing yourself to dress down when you feel more empowered in a business suit (or vice versa) may come across as fake, but if it does suit both you and the people you are meeting, then go for it. Similarly, if you are a genuine football fan, and the people you are meeting introduce the topic, by all means engage, but if your knowledge is limited and your enthusiasm vestigial, it is better to admit ignorance up front than to be exposed.

Another problem, to which many people are susceptible, is that of speech and accents. It seems to be a fundamental part of human nature that we imitate each other, especially when we are trying to get along. But if you find yourself picking up regional or national accents and phrases, restrain yourself: it can very easily be misinterpreted as sarcasm.

Remember

1. *Be on time* – never late!
2. Have a good, firm handshake.
3. Maintain eye contact.
4. Smile.
5. Use the other person's name (make the meeting personal).
6. Exchange business cards and look at them respectfully.
7. Provide appropriate, but good-quality, refreshment. If you are anticipating a lunch or other meal break, it is probably helpful to say this in advance, so that people's concentration is not unduly disturbed by the pangs of hunger.
8. Play at the best venue and organize the kick-off time.
9. Manage the first meeting by creating a powerful personal first impression.
10. Get to know the other side. Know them as people, not just opponents.
11. Keep the atmosphere warm and friendly for this first meeting.
12. Try to mirror (but that does not mean imitate) the other party and create an atmosphere of trust.

The Power of Questions

Information is crucial to the outcome of a negotiation and you should take the initiative with a well-practised and thorough questioning technique. Not only will appropriate questioning provide you with information, but the phrasing and skill used should stimulate a more open exchange of views.

Open and Closed Questions

Open questions usually begin with words such as Why, What if, How (Who, When, Where tend on balance to be the start of a closed question), but not all of these questions are open. An open question is one that cannot be answered with a simple yes or no, or indeed a longer display of 'logic' and facts: it demands more. Open questions are intended to uncover the thinking, needs and objectives of the other party, and how they feel about that. Phrasing open questions is a skill in itself, but one that can be learned and practised.

Closed questions demand a simple one-dimensional answer ('Yes', 'No', '17 September', '£3000') and if the party cannot give that, you rapidly hit a brick wall (or on a bad day a PowerPoint presentation) of facts, stats and logic, which you cannot easily challenge. You have invited him to show why something cannot be done: he has shown you. End of argument (or the beginning of a very difficult argument, unless you are absolutely confident that your 'logic' will beat his; as we discussed in earlier chapters, this is not a style of negotiation you want to get into unless you have to).

Closed questions invite your opposite to close discussion down, to limit the field, to refute your argument with (apparently) irrefutable logic, fact, corporate policies and so on. They tend to force people into corners, and although sometimes that will indeed be what you want to do (for example if you think you have discussed and agreed everything but there is a curious reluctance to sign, in which case some closed questions may force the point – they either have to give a straight answer, or walk away with nothing), usually, and especially early in negotiations, closed questions will either close off potentially profitable avenues or just get people's backs up.

Open questions require your opposite to explain things, to relate his or her objectives to yours, to explore or at least consider alternatives. The onus is then on you to listen to the answers. Expert negotiators understand the power of open questions, especially during the opening of the negotiation.

Open questions	Appropriate for	Not appropriate
How can we help you?	Encouraging discussion	When you need to be more specific
What are your reasons for …?	Gaining more information	

Closed questions usually demand a simple yes or no answer. They are useful for establishing specific points of fact and can assist in summarizing, when you are going through various points to clarify the situation or what has been agreed.

Closed questions	Appropriate for	Not appropriate
Can you deliver by the 17th?	Checking specific facts	Gaining general information
Is this what you suggested?	Clarifying the situation	If you do not want a no answer

Closed questions are often asked at the conclusion of the negotiation. The ultimate closed selling question is 'Will you buy it?' and this is the reason why salespeople avoid closed questions so avidly.

If you ask a closed question in a sales environment and receive a positive reply, then the problem is solved. If, however, the answer is 'no' then you are at a disadvantage. Only ask a closed question if you can live with a negative answer. You may prefer to follow the route of salespeople and try to close the other party with an alternative method. The choice would be 'How much discount can you give me?' rather than 'Can you give me a discount?'

Probing Questions

Such questions are usually used to clarify points of detail and are normally open questions directed to a specific subject. Some excellent probes are not actually questions but statements such as 'Please, tell me more.' You can choose whether to probe by making a statement or by asking a question that can validate or expand on the information you already have.

Probing questions	Appropriate for	Not appropriate
What specific tests do you use to ensure consistent quality?	Checking information already obtained	If exploring personal information – care will be needed
Why do you say that?	Tying down the other party and making them give you the information you require	

Leading Questions

Leading questions indicate the answer that is expected. Note that these are generally inadmissible in courts of law (the classic is allegedly 'When did you stop beating your partner?' which gives even an innocent defendant nowhere to go!). But they are totally fair in a commercial negotiation.

They vary in character, but often either you are essentially asking the other party to commit, or they have to back-track from or qualify the position you have already reached (and no-one wants to do that).

Leading questions	Appropriate for	Not appropriate
So there will be no problem in meeting our quality requirements?	Gaining acceptance of your views	Obtaining information on how the other party feels
These prices will remain fixed for 23 months, won't they?	Tying down the other party and making them give you the information you require	

Reflective Questions

Such questions are a powerful means of expressing your own, and obtaining information about the other person's feelings. They often appear as statements without a question mark, but clearly require a response from the other person indicating how they feel.

Reflective questions	Appropriate for	Not appropriate
'You seem unhappy about that proposal'	Encouraging the other person to continue talking and to look deeper into a situation	Checking facts
'That seems to cause you a problem'		

It is relatively easy to phrase closed questions and they can be very effective in establishing facts and information. Open questions can be seen as encouraging discussion and seeking the other person's opinions in an unprejudiced way. You should attempt to use a combination of types of questions at different points of the negotiation.

For example:

Seller – 'I believe you were late in payment for the last order we delivered. Is that correct?' (Closed)

Buyer – 'Yes.'

Seller – 'What were the reasons for this?' (Open)

Buyer – 'We had some staffing problems within our accounting systems department.'

Seller – 'You feel that things were particularly difficult at that time.' (Reflective)

Buyer – 'Yes, a couple of systems had failed and we hadn't got the appropriate staff to deal with it.'

Seller – 'So what did you do about it?' (Probing)

Effective questioning skills involve asking the appropriate questions at the appropriate times. Excessive use of closed questions, for example, may close the meeting down at the very point where you want to encourage the other person to talk about a particular issue.

Hypothetical Questions

Hypothetical questions are another powerful type of question which can be used to good effect in a negotiation. These questions usually begin 'What if ...' or 'Suppose ...'. They are useful for getting the other party to think about new ideas, and are especially helpful in breaking deadlock situations. They enable various options to be tabled for discussion but free from any commitment. For example:

'What if we extended the contract to two years?'

'Suppose we made you our sole supplier?'

Creativity is a powerful tool and characterizes the skilled negotiator. Hypothetical questions provide one way of introducing creativity.

Multiple Questions

These are usually a string of questions asked as one, for example:

'How do you ensure fixed prices, delivery, quality and the level of after-sales service we require?'

Multiple questions are useful for putting the other party under pressure; but make sure that you get multiple answers. Often the other party will just sit back and answer part of the question, usually at length, that suits them best, or to which they have the ready answer, or which to them (but not necessarily to you) seems the most important. Alternatively, they may simply get confused and give a single but partial answer to the several points.

Multiple questions may be unavoidable because independent factors interact. You may need to ask 'If we take product option C, but only the volumes in our first request, but on the delivery schedule we suggested in our second, but we give you preferred supplier status for next year's product launch, how do you feel?' It is a valid and necessary multiple question, but the honest answer may well be 'confused', possibly to the point where he or she has to abandon the meeting to seek instruction and guidance!

If you ask each question separately it will carry more weight and will force the other party to answer each part in turn. If you do need to ask a multiple question, you need to keep a mental note of the separate elements, and the extent to which each has been addressed in the response. Always bear in mind that the best result on each individual question may not add arithmetically to the best achievable overall result, and so multiple questions may sometimes be necessary.

Remember

1. Plan your questions in advance.
2. Concentrate on open questions at the beginning of meetings.
3. When you find something interesting, probe.
4. Make sure that you write down all important facts.
5. If you want commitment ask a closed question.

The Skill of Listening

There is little point in asking open questions and probing deeply if you are not listening carefully for the answers at the same time. How did you get on with the listening test in Chapter 5?

Expert negotiators know how important it is to practise good listening skills (Figures 10.1 and 10.2). These are skills that can be learned and used. Hearing is not listening. Listening needs effort and can be hard work.

Encourage the Other Party to Talk

The more that people talk the more they give away. A good listener is able to gather a great deal of information when confronted by a talkative person across the table. Encourage them to talk.

Remember also what represents many people's most popular subject: themselves! People will talk endlessly about their hobbies, families, car, holidays, and so on, if prompted. All of the information may prove useful. Keep a record of what is said (even to the point of maintaining a file on each contact you deal with). It may not be

Reflecting	Let me see if I've got your point …
Supporting	Are you saying …?
Supporting	Yes, good idea. And then?
Disagreeing	Won't that cost too much?
Constructing	Would it help if we …? What would you like to happen?
Criticizing	If we do this for him, we'll have to do it for everybody else. (but carefully!)
Clarifying	Isn't the point that …?
Interpreting	Are you suggesting …?
Confirming	So, we agree that …
Testing	Would it be right to say that …? If we did this then …

Figure 10.1   Some behaviours that indicate listening

Ineffective	Effective
Non-verbal behaviour Listener looks bored, uninterested or judgemental; avoids eye contact; displays distracting mannerisms (doodles, plays with a paperclip, reads papers, etc.)	Listener maintains positive posture; avoids distracting mannerisms; keeps attention focused on speaker; maintains eye contact; nods and smiles when appropriate
Focus of attention Listener shifts attention to himself; 'When something like that happens I always find that …'	Listener keeps focus of her comments on the speaker: 'When that happened what did you do?' 'How did you feel?'
Acceptance Listener fails to accept speaker's ideas and feelings: 'I think it would have been better to …'	Listener accepts ideas and feelings: 'That's an interesting idea, can you say more about it?'
Empathy Listener fails to empathize: 'I don't see why you felt that'	Listener empathizes: 'So when that happened, you felt angry'
Probing Listener fails to probe into an area, to follow up an idea or feeling	Listener probes in a helpful way (but does not cross-examine): 'Could you tell me more about that?' 'Why did you feel that way? Listener follows up: 'A few minutes ago you said that …'
Paraphrasing Listener fails to check the accuracy of communication by restating in his own words important statements made by the speaker	Listener paraphrases at the appropriate time
Summarizing Listener fails to summarize	Listener summarizes the progress of the conversation from time to time
Advice Listener narrows the range of alternatives by suggesting a 'correct' course of action	Listener broadens the range of ideas by suggesting (or asking the speaker for) a number of alternatives

Figure 10.2 Characteristics of effective listening

appropriate for you to be scribbling frantically while your visitor is chatting about her daughter's wedding, but why not have a junior or trainee in the back of the room taking notes? (Do bear in mind though that Data Protection Acts govern the collection of personal information, how you can store it and where you can disseminate it. Secretly recording negotiations is a definite no-no!)

Check the Misunderstandings

As you listen to the other side you will soon hear if there have been any misunderstandings during the first minutes of your negotiation. It may be that one of your assumptions has proved faulty or that the other party has the wrong information. Do not hesitate to correct these errors and be open and honest. There is little point in continuing a discussion if it is based on a faulty premise and cannot be taken to a proper conclusion.

However, a lot of people in business, as in other walks of life, insist on believing what they want to believe, such as the salesperson who is convinced there is a sale to be made, even after you have explained that you have just signed a contract for the next three years' supply. Some people will not take 'no' for an answer (and if they are on a commission-only basis it is hard to blame them).

More bizarrely, some people will not take 'yes' for an answer either: you are happy with the price, the quality, the delivery; you have said you will get your people to draft a contract, and still they go on, remaking the sale to which you have already consented. This requires the patience of Job, rather than any trainable negotiating skill.

Active Listening Skills

- Listen to what others have to say in order to understand what they mean.

- Listen to what others have put into their idea (look for positives).

- By listening you are more able to identify skills in other people.

- By listening you are able to gain a clearer picture of what is in somebody's mind, so you are able to respond.

- When listening put your own thoughts to the back of your mind in order to understand the other person's point of view.

- By attentive listening you are able to make better use of time by quicker understanding.

- Lack of listening will demotivate others, particularly where the boss doesn't listen.

- By listening you will be able to recall valuable information.

- By listening you show consideration and respect for others.

- By listening you gain or improve your authority.

- By listening you will improve the level of influence you have.

One of the best listening skills is the use of summary. When you summarize you are checking your understanding and at the same time gaining control over the conversation.

The Power of Summary

Perhaps the best way to summarize is to repeat back to the other party what they have just said. If you use an expression like, 'So what you are saying is ...' you will be able to check that you have heard and understood the key points. In these modern times it is particularly useful if you have the ability to strip out the jargon and management-speak. The 'techie' stuff may have to go back into the actual contract, but if you and your opposite cannot define what you have agreed in relatively simple English (or whatever your language of negotiation may be) there is little chance of the people who draft the legal contract successfully alighting on the core issues of the proposed deal.

Using the Telephone

The principles of listening are even more important on the telephone. When eye-to-eye contact is broken the use of words becomes paramount. Earlier in the chapter we mentioned the surprising preponderance of body language in our understanding of what people say and mean, and the telephone deprives us of that essential input. Instead, we have to rely on use of language and tone of voice: if your interlocutor is, for example, not a first language English speaker, or has a regional accent with which you are unfamiliar, or is awkward on the telephone precisely because he, like you, is missing the visual cues, there is a wide scope for misunderstanding.

The same applies even more if you are using VOIP (voice over Internet protocol), which can have bizarre delays, and video-conferencing where, although you can to some extent see the other party, quite often the perceived body language does not quite match the words. Subconsciously, we are almost bound to see or hear people in these conditions as being shifty or untrustworthy. Due allowance must be made (especially since they are probably viewing you in the same way).

Expert negotiators do not enjoy using the telephone to make important decisions. It is vital to be able to look into the other party's eyes at key moments. Our advice is to try to meet face to face wherever possible.

A strong case can stand up to an exchange of words but is sometimes diluted when negotiators can see each other. When two sides can see each other they tend to move together. On the telephone the apparently stronger case can often prevail.

A telephone call, however, can be a useful means of conditioning the other party concerning a price rise or a change of expectations. As there is no eye contact it is easier to tell lies on the telephone, so be careful that you are not manipulated into a difficult position by somebody who will not stop talking and let you interrupt. Interrupting is difficult on the telephone, so be wary of the long speech.

Certainly, do not leave a telephone call without a thorough summary of what has been agreed. It is very easy to misunderstand what you thought you heard. If any sort of agreement has been, even provisionally, agreed, ask the other party to confirm in writing (or email) or undertake to do this yourself. There are such things as verbal contracts.

The New Media

If telephones can be problematic in negotiation, the email and related technologies are arguably even worse.

Email is all-pervasive and, given the globalization of supply chains, pretty well unavoidable. As a method of sending and receiving information it is phenomenal, but as a medium over which to conduct a negotiation, there are some big problems.

Not the least is the sheer informality of email. It is an instant medium – unmediated, often, by secretaries or PAs, and it is very easy for busy people to fire off messages without reading them through or considering their likely effect on the recipient.

Then there is the informality of language. 'Got yr qOt: LOL' (I received your quotation and laughed out loud') may not be the ideal business communication, especially since the other party doesn't know whether you are laughing or not!

There are also some very obvious, but all too common, traps. One involves sending a counter-party an excerpt from a document to support your position, but inadvertently attaching the entire document! By all means send the paragraphs starting 'We believe the justification for rejecting the proposed price increase is …', but try not to include the next paragraph which starts 'We don't think our suppliers will accept this because …'!

Another very nasty trap is the 'Reply All' key. You will often be negotiating with two or more potential suppliers; one misclick of the mouse and everyone knows their rivals' negotiating position.

My advice would be, whenever you are emailing anything of substance to the negotiation, to create it as you would a formal business letter, and then send as an attachment. Even 'snail mail' can go wrong (the wrong letters in the wrong envelope, for example), but this discipline does give you a few more opportunities to consider your position and, more importantly, how you are going to convey it most effectively to the other party.

Consider the Other Person

It may well be that you are not immediately attracted by the quality, content or style of the other person. Never let this show. You must maintain a professionally positive outlook and keep the conversation moving.

Remember one of the key elements of negotiation: the more people like you the more they will give you; the more they dislike you the easier they will find it to say no.

The Power of Silence

Never underestimate the power of silence. Be aware of the effect it can have on the other party if you sit and say nothing. It can be most threatening and difficult to endure (see Scenario 10 in Chapter 13 and 'A silent rector' in Chapter 5).

A good maxim is to say nothing if you have nothing to say. Sit, listen, gain information and then ask questions. This will net you enormous advantages (although the power of silence doesn't work too well on the phone, as people may just think they have lost the connection).

Remember

1. Signals are often in what is not said, and on the telephone you cannot see the other party.
2. A large amount of information is obtained through observation and it is easier for people to be misleading on the telephone.
3. It will take longer to say what is necessary on the telephone.
4. It is a useful way of avoiding compromise because the use of such increases with physical proximity.
5. Look interested and encourage people to talk, especially about themselves.
6. Listening is an active skill that needs to be practised. If the medium allows, looking is at least as important.
7. Make people feel that you are interested in them and their business.
8. Use silence as a powerful conversational tool.
9. Avoid the telephone wherever possible for important negotiations.
10. Be very wary of email.

Managing Movement

Who Moves First?

A great many definitions of negotiation contain the word 'movement'. A negotiation involves movement or change towards an agreement that is seen as beneficial to each party.

This does not mean, however, that the process of movement has to be bilateral. Two-way movement is a perfectly proper process but the key point to make here is that you should only contemplate moving once you have exhausted the means by which you can get the other party to move on their own.

What we are searching for here are approaches that will cause the other party to move towards us before we have to consider moving towards them. There are three approaches or styles of negotiating that are likely to cause unilateral movement from the other party:

■ emotion

■ logic

■ threat.

These were covered in Chapters 1 and 2, where we created your negotiating profile. It may now be opportune to revisit your profile scores to check which of these three you use most often and, more importantly, most effectively. Let me recap briefly.

Emotion

Emotion is a powerful means of moving people. Advertising agencies use it above all other methods to move us to make a purchase.

If you can arrange the feelings of the other party in such a way to cause them to move towards you then you have found the power of emotion. Words such as sympathy, love, envy, pity, delight, friendship and care are all associated with ways of leveraging some movement from others.

Logic

If you have a powerful argument and you time its use well you have every chance of persuading the other party to move unilaterally.

During the preparation phrase you will have prepared your ideas, gathered evidence and been ready for counter-arguments, so nothing here should take you by surprise. This is the opening stage of the negotiation and gives you the opportunity to state your case and offer your reasoning, evidence and statistical proof.

The key to this early stage of negotiation is to ensure that your case and logical reasoning take precedence. Make sure that you are saying 'why' before the other party is saying 'why not'. Get your reasons in first. It is more difficult to counter an argument when the other party has already gained momentum. Most will vigorously defend a position they take, and it is often easier to defend an entrenched position than to attack it.

Accordingly, never give the other side the chance to lay out their reasons and logical arguments. Be careful about asking the other negotiator 'why' they believe what they said is true, or 'why' they are putting up their prices. All that you will receive is a barrage of justification from a well-prepared adversary.

You may well find that the other party will move unilaterally towards your position courtesy of your powerful and well-timed case of logical reasoning, but be aware that your display of logic almost demands a riposte: you need to be very sure that not just the facts of your 'logical' case, but the way they are linked, hang together and are really watertight. From your point of view, your opponent's 'facts' may well be unassailable, but they may not be relevant to the case, or the logic that links them to, for example, a request for a price rise, may be faulty.

To give an example, most of us are conditioned to the idea that greater volumes should equate to lower unit price (see Chapter 7). But suppose you insist on this 'logic' to your supplier, and they in turn point out that the existing plant is already running at full capacity: to install a new line, for your order of a product exclusive to you, which you are only guaranteeing for 12 months, requires additional capital expenditure which is bound to be reflected in the unit price. So their 'logic' demands that you accept a price rise! Now there may be many ways in which an ultimately successful negotiation could proceed from there, but beating each other up over numbers is unlikely to be a successful strategy for either party.

Threat

Threat may be seen as the counter-balance to emotion. If emotion feeds on love then threat feeds on fear.

It may be possible to generate unilateral movement from the other side if they are sufficiently fearful of a negative outcome. This has to be done skilfully otherwise a great deal of bad feeling can be generated which can subsequently cause grief.

Subtle use of threat consists of the potential withdrawal of business, loss of opportunities, or the inability to sign a larger order. Quite often threat is cloaked in words such as: 'It would be a great shame ...' or 'I hope that you won't make me ...'

Always consider the subtle use of threat and rarely use it explicitly. It can be a powerful persuader but at the same time it needs careful implementation.

Now it's your Turn to Move/Place the Marker

Once you have done your preparation well, you will know exactly what parameters you have for movement: both upper and lower levels. Normally you will go into a negotiation with some room to manoeuvre. It is difficult to do so with absolutely no room to move. It may seem fatuous to point out that your movement is supposed to be towards your objectives, but it is worth mentioning only because often you will have multiple objectives, and it may be permissible or even essential to move away from a minor objective (providing you are still within the allowable parameters) if that is likely to obtain a greater benefit on a major objective. Conversely, there may be no merit at all in securing terms on say delivery, payment and quality that far exceed your expectations if your company's situation is that only an immediate price reduction is of any real benefit.

What is important now is to apply these parameters skilfully so that you do not have to walk away because you were unrealistic or pay too much because you started too high.

First, look at your numbers and calculate what your opening bid will be. It has to be aimed high enough to secure a good deal (the more you ask for the more you are likely to get) but not so high that your credibility will be damaged. Your knowledge of the market will help you to put down your first marker in the best place.

Beware if you are buyer or seller – how much do you really know about the market?

Once that marker is down it remains down and cannot be removed. You must, therefore, delay placing the marker as long as possible and when you do place it, place it with care.

When a car salesperson asks 'What do you want for your car?', answer 'What are you prepared to offer?'

Do not even think of making an offer or placing a marker until you have exhausted all one-way movement possibilities.

Certainly you should try to force the other party to place their marker first. In a buying or selling situation the buyer always has the advantage in as much as the seller will have a price list or may have put down a price in the tender documents. You may be pleasantly surprised that their aspirations are less than you expected and you can tune your deal accordingly. Be prepared to experience a rat-a-tat:

'I need a discount.'
'How much are you looking for?'
'What can you offer me?'
'Give me a clue.'
'I don't know, you're the expert …'

This is the legitimate counter-play of two good negotiators. Obviously someone will have to put down a marker eventually, but try to make sure it is not you. It may be useful, although it takes some skill, to convince the other side that you have some fixed and rigid parameters within which you are working, but without disclosing exactly what they are.

How to Move

Once you decide to move you must move only in the smallest of increments. Again, plan the size of the steps that you will take. Remember also that you must try never to move unilaterally. That is what you want the other party to do! If you move try to receive something in return for your move: 'If you do … then I will …' is the script.

If ... Then ...

Once you move you have advertised the fact that you can move. You are also allowing the assumption that you may have more movement to offer. Therefore never give anything away for nothing. You must trade your moves, not give them away, and always move in the smallest possible increments. Remember, you are bargaining, not compromising (see earlier). The increments you offer should also be of decreasing size. This acts as a disincentive to the other party to continue asking for more: they are as aware as you of the law of diminishing returns and they will not normally want to jeopardize a deal for a few hundredths of a percentage point, certainly not for something that is less than their own margin of error on their costings (which may be remarkably large).

You must also remember that if there is no pressure to move then don't. Concessions are only valued when they are won. If you move too easily you are only encouraging the other party to raise their expectations for further movements.

When the Other Party Moves

You should always promote in the other party a willingness to make concessions. Try to convince them that their current position is untenable, that they will not lose face if they do move, or that you may reciprocate the move yourself if they go first.

When you are offered something in a negotiation get into the habit of immediately saying 'thank you' and moving on. It is discourteous not to thank someone for something they have given you. It is also a common human trait that if someone looks or sounds ungrateful you are much more likely not to offer any more. And do make a note of where you have got to so far, and let the other side see that you have taken note. They will know that they cannot go back on that position later.

Even if what you are offered is not ultimately what you want, bank it and go for more.

If a concession is offered on something you do not want, encourage it, value it and then ask for a concession in the area you want to be in. Refusing a concession outright is poor practice. Banking it to trade back later is good practice.

Best Concession Behaviour

A concession presents you with three problems:

- Should I make it now?
- How much ground should I give?
- What am I going to get in return?

Remember

1. Try to make the other party move unilaterally.
2. Emotion, logic and threat are powerful means of one-way movement.
3. Be prepared and understand your case, and the factors that are more or less likely to drive your opponent.
4. Get your logic in first, but only if it is unassailable. An accumulation of costs, prices and other numbers is not the same thing as a logical argument.
5. Be careful asking the question 'Why?'
6. Threat needs careful handling.
7. Do not threaten people. Threaten deals.
8. Do not make threats that are not credible, or that you are not prepared to carry out.
9. Plan your opening bid carefully.
10. Be reluctant to put your marker down first.
11. Move in small steps only and as creatively as possible.
12. Move only in reaction to a movement from the other party.
13. Never give anything away – trade it.
14. Always say 'thank you' and go for more.
15. Always bank their concessions – even if a concession is worthless to you, it may have some value traded back to them.

Trading and Dealing

This is the part of negotiation with which most people are familiar. Quite a few readers will have cheated by turning straight to this section in search of instant tips, and I can only urge them to turn back and read the preceding chapters which explain how you can create the context in which your bargaining and trading is going to be most effective. The fact that 'bargaining and dealing' comes late in my description of how expert negotiators work only shows how wide the gulf is between the expert and the novice. It shows how reluctant the expert is to move unless all possibility of getting the other side to move unilaterally has been exhausted.

The Language of Bargaining

Bargaining becomes a much easier process when an effective script is used. The key expression is 'if I do X for you, then I want Y in return.' I give you something in return for what you give me. If you have planned it correctly then you will be giving the other party something that costs you little in return for something that you value greatly.

Exchanging Variables

In Chapter 9 (Figure 9.2) we looked at just a selection of the huge number of variables that could be brought into play in a negotiation. For any particular negotiation, some of these will be inappropriate or irrelevant, others will be non-negotiable (either it's in the deal or there is no deal, and you *must* remember not to start trading the non-negotiable elements), but there will still be many left and these can often be subdivided and salami-sliced almost ad infinitum. We also pointed out that you need to have a very good idea of how much each of these variables, in their smallest tradable increments, are worth to you, positively if you are receiving a concession, negatively if you are conceding. Note that those are not necessarily + and – the same number, nor is the graph necessarily linear: a further, even generous, concession to you in an area where you already have a pretty good deal may not be worth much to you, but for you to concede from that position *on the same variable* could be quite costly. For example, if you are in a servicing industry and your existing arrangements for ordering and receiving spares already allow you to offer faultless next-day service, a further improvement in your supplier's delivery times may not get you any additional business, but an equivalent drop in delivery performance might cost you a lot of custom. You need to know intimately the cost (in the broadest sense) implications of any variable increment in either direction.

You also need at least to attempt to value these variables from the other party's point of view. A good example is the trading of payment terms. If the other party has cash-flow problems and a large overdraft they may be prepared to reward you much more than the cost of the money if you can pay them promptly. They will receive something that they value highly and will be prepared to reward you accordingly. It may be that you are a cash-rich company for whom early payment is not important. You have therefore obtained a first class trade: extra discount in return for early payment. The other party is also happy because they have secured their cash flow.

You can then move on to the next bargain – in a complex deal the number of variables to be traded often reaches double figures. So the process starts over again: 'What will you give me if I can help you with …'

As I have already said, remember that you should never refuse anything offered to you. It may be that you are seeking a larger discount than the one offered or that the payment terms are not quite right, but you should never reject anything outright. It is important to learn a script that includes sentences like 'Thank you for that. It's certainly a step in the right direction', or 'Thank you for the discount. It's not quite what we need but I appreciate you making the move towards me.' Both of these statements give you ownership of what has been offered but also make it very clear that more is required.

If you reject something that is offered to you the other party can always take it back. You should encourage the other party to move because once they have moved it is much easier for them to move again.

Many times novice negotiators disdain concessions from the other side. If you have a sour expression and a rejecting tone of voice the concession will be withdrawn and the likelihood of your receiving something similar will be reduced. Bear in mind also that some concession you disdain may actually be the fruits of the other party working at or even past the limits of their authority. If they have risked and sweated to offer you something, even if it is not what you want, do not fling it back in their faces.

Negotiating with One Variable

The settling of differences when there is only one variable at issue is known as compromise. There may genuinely be only one question (typically, but not always, price) that is open for discussion. Equally, it may be that all other issues have been set in stone in previous negotiations which cannot be reopened, and there is just one outstanding issue (which can happen, for example, when someone has forgotten some crucial element in an otherwise successful negotiation, typically a little unimportant detail like the delivery date. It is easily done!).

We saw with the early payment scenario that for bargaining to work successfully there has to be more than one variable. In that case there were two variables: early payment and extra discount.

When negotiation comes down to one variable, and especially when there is likely to be a log jam with that last one, a compromise becomes useful. It is the settling of differences within one set of parameters.

The best known and most obvious compromise is the 50:50 split. This is an easy way of settling differences. It is, however, almost too easy and is a soft option that expert negotiators avoid.

When faced with a potential compromise expert negotiators will demand far more than a mere 50:50 split. They will start at 99 to 1 and move from there. As was said with bargaining, never give anything away. Why give 50 per cent away just to settle the deal? Perhaps 20 per cent might settle it just as easily.

I had a Spanish grandmother, and if she asked me to go to the local shop I would ask her for 10 pesetas; she would offer 1 peseta, to which I would reply:

'Come on Grandmother, compromise.'

She would then offer her compromise, which would be 2 pesetas!

Compromise is the behaviour of last resort. When you use it be just as rigorous as you would be with any other part of the deal. Remember that a compromise favours the party that aims highest (see Chapter 7, Figure 7.1).

Compromise occurs most often in face-to-face negotiations and is not as readily used during telephone negotiations. One of the reasons for this is that it takes a lot longer to say something on a telephone. Hence, the negotiation is slowed down, whereas compromises are normally quick. (The same applies to email, perhaps even more so as it is often unclear whether the other party is stalling for time, seeking advice or just has not opened his or her inbox lately.)

Remember

1. Value the variables from both sides.
2. Try to give a little and get a lot.
3. When offered something say 'thank you' and go for more.
4. Find out what the other party needs most and make them pay for it.
5. Compromise as rarely and as late as possible.
6. 50:50 is not the only compromise.
7. Aim as high as possible at the beginning if you are possibly going to use a compromise approach later.

The End of the Road

Conclusion

As you move towards the end of the negotiation it sooner or later becomes obvious that it is time to reach a conclusion. Ideally, this will be because all the relevant points have at least provisionally been agreed; often it may be that there are residual points, not crucial to your objectives, that are just not worth the time and effort to sweat over (so compromise or even just accept). Sometimes the end becomes clear because the size of the concessions being offered and traded becomes smaller and smaller.

It can, unfortunately, also be that one or both parties simply has to 'walk away'. That is inevitably going to feel like 'failure', but it is better to 'fail' now, when no money or commitment has been exchanged, than to end up walking away from an unworkable or unsatisfactory deal later on, with all the attendant claims and counter-claims, not to mention lawyers' fees.

Assuming, though, that negotiation appears to have reached an endpoint without irretrievable breakdown, at this stage you have to ascertain whether the other party has any more room to move or is, in fact, standing on the edge of the cliff ready to fall over. They may be calculating the same for you.

Watch out for brinkmanship. You can never be sure whether the other player is bluffing.

Your task then is to convince the other side that you have given them all that is on offer and if that is not sufficient either you will have to walk away or they will have to moderate their target (that is, of course, a threat and therefore must be credible).

You can add to your leverage by using a range of tactics to convince the other side of your inability to move: here are just three and a more detailed review of tactics follows in Chapter 11.

1. I've exceeded my authority

You can find a series of reasons why you cannot move any further. Blame your low budget this year, the bank manager, company policy, etc. This needs to be credible: given the power of search engines and the ready availability of reports from the likes of S&P, Moody and Experian, it can happen that your opponent has a better, or at least more rounded idea of your company's position than you do!

Be very careful that you do not mention your boss. To do so leaves you open to the other party suggesting that they talk to your boss directly. It also undermines your authority and credibility in being able to agree the deal.

2. This will cost me my job

Use emotion to persuade the other side that you have already gone further than you should have. This has to be done skilfully otherwise you can harm your credibility. (And a skilled salesperson may well be making similar representations to you. Remember that if the deal does not go through, or fails in performance, the buyer's job loss is hypothetical: if the deal fails, the salesperson's loss of bonus is often very real and immediate. You have some advantage there.)

3. I'll have to reduce my order

Do not try to obtain any further movement from the other side. You reduce what you can offer in return for what they have put on the table. (It may not be the order quantity per se; it may be the hopes you have held out of involvement in future product development, or of being a preferred supplier on some other deal, or of the right to use your company's reputation in publicity: there are many intangible benefits that may have been in play. Be wary, however, of appearing to withdraw benefits or concessions that clearly cost you little and where the withdrawal might look more like a fit of pique.)

Success in this area of negotiation always conditions the other party to accept what is on the table and to be satisfied that they could not have achieved any more.

Shaking Hands

As the end of the negotiation moves into view you need to be prepared either to make an alternative offer or to accept the offer on the table. This presumes that you have not decided to call it a day, i.e. go elsewhere.

In the sales environment this is the most important phase. The seller has worked through the sales process and now has to 'close'. This is the aspect of selling most written about and feared. It is the moment of truth when the customer says 'yes' or 'no'. There is no avoiding that ultimate closed question.

Salespeople are taught how to close out the deal. Buyers are less well trained but protect themselves with processes that stop the seller from reaching this stage. Tendering in theory allows the buyer to choose which deal to take unencumbered by the pressure of an enthusiastic salesperson or a negotiation, but in practice there is almost always some degree of post-tender negotiation, however controversial that may be.

In general, the fast shaking of hands favours the seller. Salespeople wish to make the deal and get out before any second thoughts can interfere. Ultimately, whichever side you are on if you think that it is time to agree it is better to say so and shake on the deal. Unfortunately some buyers suffer from endless doubts and these can cause the loss of a good deal.

You do need, at this stage above all others, to believe both in yourself and in the authority that has been vested in you.

You also need to recognize that no deal is 100 per cent perfect, for either side. There was always another concession to be won, another fraction of a percentage point. But the law of diminishing returns applies: it's not quite a Pareto analysis (I would be profoundly disappointed in any reader who settled for just the easy 80 per cent of the objective) but at the same time anyone who offers you 100 per cent of your original best case objectives probably does not understand the situation (so you need to ask some searching questions of yourself: 'Have I misrepresented what we need, or is this guy so desperate that he will sign for business even if his company cannot, or has no intention of, fulfilling it?').

Hard Sell, Hard Deals

Pressuring people may be fine in the one-off sale and negotiation but there is little point in tricking someone into making a potentially poor deal if you have to visit them again the next week or month.

Once people have had a chance to reflect on a deal they will soon form an opinion of whether it was to their advantage or not. If they feel that they have been tricked or manipulated they will become resentful and will seek to annul the deal or look for revenge the next time the business opportunity arises. In the limit, a truly coercive negotiation (e.g. unreasonable use of threats, especially personal threats) may allow a court to annul any ensuing contract.

Good long-term relationships must be at the forefront of most deals. Treat people with respect and they will be happy to deal again.

Written Evidence

No matter how professional the negotiators, the deal must be recorded on paper. It is at this time that misunderstandings will be ironed out and final numbers agreed. Details that were left 'on the backburner' need to be clarified, the 'non-negotiable' or 'understood' elements need to be reincorporated and the final terms and conditions signed off.

It is always worth getting a fax or preliminary copy initialled as quickly as possible in order to show that final details are agreed. It is worth racing a bit to get your version of events and agreements up-front; there can often be quite reasonable differences of interpretation and if your version is first in, that is likely to be the one that stands.

Managing the People

At the final stages of a deal it is possible to strengthen relationships ready for the next round, next time. Never underestimate the importance of this stage. I have shown how first impressions can be important and the feelings at the end are equally so.

The other party should be thanked for their professional participation. You may, where appropriate, seek to offer some symbol of the agreement: buying lunch, a drink, or signing the deal with a commemorative pen. Make the other party feel good about doing business with you and happy about dealing with you personally. But you need to have regard to your own, your employer's, and where appropriate your professional association's code of ethics. That applies equally if the other party offers, now or later, a gift. If in doubt, especially on the receipt of gifts, take advice from your superiors; at the very least, ensure that gifts and hospitality of any significance are reported. (Very few people have ever been sacked for accepting a bottle of Scotch from a supplier, but quite a lot have been sacked for concealing the fact or for lying about it.)

No matter how well you believe the deal has gone you must never show triumph. Shouts of 'result!' as the pen hits the paper are not guaranteed to foster good lasting relationships.

Bear in mind that in any deal something that is not earned is not valued. Make the other party feel that they have had to work really hard to get the deal. They will value it more.

Expert negotiators are never satisfied. They are perpetually concerned by the possibility that they have left money on the table. As we have discussed earlier, you will never know how near to the edge of the cliff you were. That is the joy or the pain of negotiating.

You should always walk away from a negotiation with a feeling that you could have got more. 'I wonder if he would have given me an extra 1 per cent if I had pushed him harder' are the words that should be in your head. If you leave a negotiation smiling with the thought that you have had a good result, just ask yourself if you really pushed as hard as you could. Did you go for the 'Wow!'?

I am not suggesting that negotiators are a breed of malcontents. Your thoughts should be towards obtaining the highest levels that are available. Be a keen, friendly negotiator with high targets.

Expert negotiators do not readily take 'no' for an answer. They will check it out, ask you to validate your ideas, revisit your evidence, question you again and then they might start to think that 'no' is a faint possibility.

'If you don't ask you don't get' is a well-worn cliché but nonetheless is a major theme for negotiators.

An expert negotiator needs to look at two different aspects of a negotiation: the task at hand and the people involved – the business and the personal dimensions. The combination that has stood the test of time is to be tough on the deal and warm towards the people. Graphically this can be represented as shown in Figure 4.1 (Chapter 4). The tick represents the preferred style area. This style is rigorous on the numbers and the money but friendly towards the people.

Unfortunately, far too many negotiators adopt a cold/tough attitude. This will achieve deals but by no means the quality of deals that a warmer approach would achieve.

Salespeople are often quite different. Many of them are so afraid that they will lose the deal that they adopt a warm/easy approach. This gains them the sale but never really puts money on the bottom line.

Remember

1. When you plan always know how far you can go. Do not be carried away in the heat of the moment.
2. Always try to know how far the other party can move. Where is their real walk-away position?
3. Try to convince the other player that you have exhausted your store of concessions and that you are unable to move any further.
4. If necessary you can start either offering back previously agreed, banked concessions (that are of little value to you) against an agreement to sign the deal off; alternatively, you can start withdrawing minor concessions that you have provisionally offered to encourage signing (but this latter needs great care, lest your counterpart starts believing that you are acting in less than good faith. It is probably something best avoided).
5. Do not trust to memory, write it down.
6. Make the final agreement a pleasant experience.
7. Make the other party feel that they have 'earned' the deal.
8. Do not show triumph.
9. Try to build the basis for a long-term relationship if appropriate.

11

Tactics and Ploys

Adopt behaviour to enhance or defend your position.

The dictionary defines tactics as 'a procedure calculated to gain some end'. If we look more closely at the dictionary definitions a number of key words can be identified. The word 'calculated' implies care in the choice of those approaches to be used, and we also need to consider the timing of their use. The word 'skilful' emphasizes the need for expertise acquired through practice and experimentation, and the word 'art' suggests that training and experience are needed to be able to make optimum use of the tactics and ploys available to you. See Chapter 7 for the consequences of brinkmanship used unskilfully.

This chapter details a number of tactics that can be used in negotiations, but they need to be used with discretion. They need to be matched to your objectives, and to the character and personality of the person you are dealing with. You certainly do not want to get stuck in a rut, routinely, unthinkingly and predictably using just those methods that you are most comfortable with, or which have worked in the past.

No general rules can be laid down about tactics. Each negotiation must be considered separately before you decide which tactics are appropriate. It is equally essential to consider the personalities and approaches of the other party or parties to the negotiation: as has been stated earlier, *people* negotiate, not companies. A particular tactic will work better on some people than others. The same tactics will work differently on the same person in different circumstances or at different times.

I have divided the list of tactics which follows into four separate sections: A, B, C and D. A represents those tactics that will help to create movement, B those that will buy you time to deal with the unexpected and cope with pressure, C those that will help you to stage-manage the negotiation and variables therein, and D those that I consider are better called tricks of the trade. The list is not definitive and readers may well have others of their own. If this is the case, write them down and try to be objective about those you use successfully and those you use less well. Because these tactics and ploys are going to be used on *people*, whose personalities vary enormously, it is essential to study the *person* you are going to negotiate with.

In buyer/seller situations, sellers have traditionally been better equipped; they understand the need to know the *person* with whom they are going to negotiate. Most sellers keep detailed notes on their customers, listing likes and dislikes, interests, family details, together with a pen-picture of each customer's personality. They are then in a better position to choose the most appropriate tactic for the person and situation. It is rare to find buyers keeping any such details about the sellers that they meet. Partly this is because buying departments tend to be collegiate, at least in terms of remuneration: if there is a bonus scheme it is likely to be shared out, and the rewards for pooling information with colleagues are small. Salespeople, by contrast, tend to hunt alone; their research and information gathering give them an edge and they see the benefits in their pay packets.

Study the other party, list the tactics that they use and work out counter-measures. Bear in mind that most tactics, while they may offer you an advantage, also entail some risk.

Above all, *do not be predictable*.

Section A: Movement Tactics

Building block technique. This can be used in several ways. You may request a price for only part of your actual requirements and in the face-to-face negotiation request prices for various quantities up to your actual needs. The other party will give ground more readily when you are raising their expectations.

If you are prepared to enter into a three-year contract, negotiate hard for a one-year contract and then ask what they would offer in addition if you went to two years. Having obtained further concessions, ask what they would offer for three years. You should get even more. But if you go straight from one year to three years the concession you might have got for two years will be transferred to the three-year contract and the concession you might have got for three years disappears!

Some people ask for prices for quantities higher than those they require and then try to get the same price for the actual lower quantity. If this approach is used, then in a buy/sell situation the seller will feel cheated and resentful. He will feel 'cold' towards the buyer. The buyer's tactic might succeed once, but he will have lost the respect of the seller and the seller will look for ways to redress the balance in future. Moving to higher quantities than originally asked for encourages the seller, who sees the prospect of *more* business than expected and can probably offer lower prices because of these higher quantities. The seller feels 'warm' towards the buyer.

Russian front. You hint that failure to agree a point (perhaps major but made to look minor) will necessitate reopening the whole range of aspects previously settled. The other party either agrees or faces a much worse alternative. This is, obviously, a threat. Is your threat credible? And is there a risk that by reopening other aspects, you may actually lose previously won concessions?

Linking issues. This is a very useful tactic but it needs careful planning. It is essentially a way of creating movement by establishing a link between issues that had previously been separate. To introduce a 'contingent relationship' between two issues on which each side wants a settlement is a prime means of getting movement where there is apparent deadlock.

For example, in buying a car the seller may be persuaded to make a further concession if you stress that if you do buy that particular model you would get it serviced at that garage.

Atom bomb/Armageddon. A suggestion that a failure to concede or drop a line that has been taken will lead to catastrophic consequences, means using threats such as: 'This may only be a small order but failure to agree could affect all your business with the *group*.' Once again, this needs to be credible: if other group business involves this supplier as the sole source of proprietary equipment, the threat is not credible.

Broken record. Repeating over and over again the point or demand you are making will sometimes win because the other party gets fed up with its constant repetition, and feels that further progress is unlikely until this obstacle is removed. It emphasizes the need for persistence in negotiation and a refusal to accept 'no' at its face value without testing.

Trojan horse. Beware the Greeks bearing gifts! Be wary of the offer that seems 'too good to refuse' and look for any hidden problems or disadvantages. For example, avoid following the example of the buyer who gratefully accepted the offer of fixed prices for 12 months, only to find that the market price subsequently fell. Similarly, be wary of the 'I can only offer this price for the next month' line: it may well appear as the standard in the next price list!

Pre-emptive strike. This forestalls any prospect of negotiation. For example, 'I have an order here for 20 tons – give me a price of X and I will put your name on it!' This can sometimes panic the other party into an agreement. It is, however, dangerous: how do you know that X, whatever improvement it may be on current pricing, is really the best you can achieve? Contrarily, is X so onerous that the other party will simply walk away? In which case, have you an alternative supplier available?

Messenger. The implication is that some absent third party is responsible for the unpleasant point you are about to deliver, for example: 'I'm only telling you what the engineers say' or 'I'm under pressure to achieve a 5 per cent reduction in current prices.' You cannot be held personally responsible for the statement. It can also help in putting down a marker without being personally responsible for it. You can then more easily retreat from this position without losing credibility. This third party must be placed at a level where it would be difficult for the person with whom you are negotiating to make contact. This tactic risks the response that 'I'll get my MD to ring your MD' (or worse, play golf with him/her). If there is any risk of that you must ensure that the 'higher authority' you have invoked is fully briefed on what you are up to.

PDT: physically disturb them. You can use a variety of physical (non-violent) means to throw the other party off balance, for example:

- Lean across the table – invade their 'territory'.

- Change the normal seating pattern.

- Sit close to them.

All of these are actions that cannot be taken as hostile but can still unsettle the other party. This is *not* about being aggressive. As I noted in a previous chapter, simply remaining silent can be one of the most physically disturbing tactics of all (see 'Silence' in Section B, below).

Brinkmanship. Going right to the edge requires great skill to avoid falling over! One way is to try and get the other party to see the edge as being closer than it actually is. However, beware of bluffing: if you are going to bluff always be aware of what you will do if your bluff is called.

Deadlines. These can be imposed or agreed and can encourage parties to concentrate on creative solutions but at the same time realize that concessions are necessary. A deadline may cover the whole deal; it equally and validly may cover a partial or provisional deal: 'My engineers must have a provisional agreement on the technical aspects tonight, even if we don't close the financial terms until next week.'

Beware that imposed deadlines do not lead to precipitate solutions, and if you have yourself imposed the deadline, you cannot very easily get out of it with any credibility.

Personal favour. Essentially this is an emotive stance. Emphasize the trouble you personally went to for the other party, for example, 'I had to work hard to get the engineers to even look at your product' or 'I had to make special arrangements to get your invoices paid in the time you wanted'.

Some door-to-door sellers use this, for example, 'I only need to sell one more to win our competition'. The point is made that to ask for more or to refuse to buy would be unreasonable, or uncharitable, or downright mean. Has the salesman shown you pictures of his handicapped daughter yet?

Guilty party. Make the other party feel guilty by suggesting that they are breaking some code or agreement, or that they are refusing something already conceded by other, more reasonable people. They may make a concession to convince you that this is not the case.

Be aware, though, that they may have better and more current market knowledge than you. Business is often comprised of a set of very small circles. If you claim that 'Simpkins from Acme Holdings would give me this, why can't you?' how sure are you that Simpkins and your current opponent didn't train at the same company and aren't members of the same gym?

Salami. Feed a difficulty or 'nasty' in thin slices, piece by piece. This often produces concessions because the other party wishes to get away from an increasingly uncomfortable situation.

Dunce. Undermine the other party's faith in his case by claiming that he has not done his homework and has got his facts wrong; that he was not well briefed. If this can be demonstrated it is possible to sow seeds of doubt about matters that have been prepared and are correct, thus sapping confidence and producing a feeling of inferiority. Be careful that you can substantiate any such challenge you make or your own credibility will suffer. This tactic should (unless the errors are real and obvious) be used very sparingly, and always with the implication that it is not he or she that is the dunce, but rather their support staff, superiors, etc. Avoid lines such as 'You obviously don't understand …'; this is insulting and belittling, and forces people into a defensive or self-justifying mode. It is unlikely to get the best out of them, and even if you do reach a deal, they are likely to leave with a feeling of resentment.

An alternative, more complicit, approach, might start, 'You and I both understand that …. But how can we get your company to see things that way?' The salesperson is now on your team; he or she has been accepted into the charmed circle of those privileged with the higher understanding!

Hard/soft or Mr Nice/Mr Nasty. This is a tactic for team negotiations. One of the team makes very high demands at the start of the negotiation and indicates a firm stand. Before he loses face by having to back down, another team member takes over and indicates a willingness to take a more reasonable attitude, often to the relief of the other party, although the initial high demands have reduced their expectations.

This requires close cooperation and planning between members. If you are on the receiving end of this tactic remember that the objective of Mr Nice and Mr Nasty is exactly the same: a good deal for *them*! (Mr Nice and Mr Nasty need to remember that as well; they have the same objectives, they are not in competition to show which approach works best).

Full disclosure – openness. This depends very much on the atmosphere that has been created. Parties need to feel that they will not be exploited by the other and it can lead swiftly to an agreement which both consider good. This is often used when parties have been dealing with each other over a long period and trust has been established.

Remember – trust takes time to build but can be destroyed very easily.

Openness is demonstrated rather than stated. *Beware* of the person who uses phrases such as 'I'm now going to be totally open with you' – they seldom are!

Charity. This is an appeal to the better nature of the other party. It is essentially an emotional appeal to the other party as a person rather than as a representative of their organization. It may need a very light touch, but after all, would they want to feel responsible for the 20 lay-offs of long-serving staff, the knock-on effects on other local businesses, or even the real cutbacks in your firm's charitable and social programmes, that must inevitably happen if a satisfactory deal is not reached?

Re-escalation of demand. After conceding and moving towards the other party you may find they are unwilling to move and persist in pushing for more. You therefore indicate that you have moved too far already and must return to your original position or beyond. The other party will often agree the deal at that stage, fearing that what they have so far obtained may slip away. You need to be aware of how your original concessions were arrived at: if at some stage you have conceded that, say, rising raw material costs do form a justification for a price rise, you cannot very readily go back to a 'no increase allowed' position. They, like you, have 'thanked and banked' your concessions.

One more thing. For those who remember the American TV detective, this is the 'Colombo' tactic. This can be used at the end of the negotiation, particularly if it has taken time to get this far. A further concession may be obtained, working on the basis that the other party will not want to waste what has been agreed, and/or when time is pressing. Use care: the 'one more thing' must not be so crucial that it leads to a reopening of the whole negotiation. However, it can get you just that little bit more.

The optimistic summary. Summarize in a way that tips the balance just in your favour. If the other party does not object at the time they will appear unreasonable if they raise the issue later in the negotiation. In extended negotiations (i.e. over several meetings) always try to get your summary of 'the plot so far' in first, and couched in terms most favourable to you. The need for contemporaneous note-taking, in detail, is obvious.

Section B: Buying Time

Headache. Oh No! Not today, I've got a headache!' Essentially this is an emotional appeal not to press a point, and designed to make the other party feel it would be unreasonable to do so. Who likes to be thought unreasonable?

Casino. Suggest that the proposals made by the other party are a pure gamble and cannot be taken seriously. This can be done by using phrases such as 'You've got to be joking' or 'Pull the other one'. The implication is that if they are serious then there is no prospect of any deal whatsoever.

Remember – do this with a smile and you are unlikely to cause offence. Remember that, on the phone or by email, they cannot see your smile: they may really believe that you think they are chancers or incompetents, which is not a good basis for further negotiation.

Defence in depth. Use several levels of staff/management before the issue reaches the final decision maker. At each level it is hoped that additional information will be obtained. This must be done carefully so that you do not undermine your own authority. Statements such as 'Our normal procedure is …' can indicate that the other party will have to conform to this. Do not confuse this with the tactic 'Messenger', in Section A above.

Silence. At a recent meeting a manager had just made a superb presentation of his negotiating case to an opposing group. It was clear that the audience was impressed but an uneasy silence developed as people looked at each other to see who was going to be the first to speak. Just as one was about to ask a question the manager began going over the key points again. This happened several times.

If he had stopped talking and started listening he might have learned something!

Silence is a void and people feel an overwhelming need to fill it. However, we must learn to manage silence. If you ask a question and get an unsatisfactory answer the best thing to do is nothing at all: demand more information by remaining silent!

Many sellers, faced with silence, will go on offering concessions until they get a verbal reaction, for example: 'We could do X' – silence – 'And we could also do Y.'

Use silence but also plan what you will do if it is used on you.

Recessing. Seek an adjournment to consolidate, review and recalculate, or possibly reshape a deal. New ideas often emerge if a break is taken, preferably away from the stress of the actual negotiation. It often forces parties to reconsider their respective stances and question the reasonableness of the positions they have taken.

Recesses should always be taken when:

- some complicated calculations have to be done

- the emotional temperature is rising

- you are renegotiating as a member of a group and your act is beginning to fall apart.

It is not unknown for a deadlock to be broken while both parties are sharing a natural break.

A recess often results in a renewal of energy and concentration. However, used too often it can generate distrust, suspicion or frustration, which will hinder movement. Recesses also take time, and very often time pressures are a crucial element in negotiation.

Dumbstruck. Look astonished or even horrified, but say nothing! This puts the onus on the other party to explain or even excuse what has been said, weakening their case and also giving you time to think. More emotion is used here than in just remaining silent. You are making the other party worry that he or she has committed some huge blunder, but you are not risking the 'you cannot be serious' insult. Some people can achieve this with a single raised eyebrow.

All I can afford. This needs to be accompanied by persistence or the 'broken record' approach if the other party is to be convinced. If accepted, the result can be a mutual concentration on alternatives to enable the deal to be made within the limits stated. Do not overstate your case and lose face by having to back down.

Let's go for lunch. Deals can often be concluded when the atmosphere or surroundings are changed and a more relaxed and informal setting is substituted. This is less formal than recessing, and can be used by either party to the negotiation.

Side issue or red herring. This tactic highlights a comparatively unimportant issue so that when finally agreed the other party feels that they have 'broken the back' of the negotiation and can relax. When the real issue comes up it gets less attention, to the benefit of the party using the tactic.

Fogging. This is nothing more than pure waffle, designed to confuse the issue or buy time to consider one's own position. At the end of the negotiation you will be left wondering what the other side has said if they use this.

Deliberate misunderstanding. This is a particularly useful ploy to buy time to think after a complicated proposal, case or explanation. 'Could you just run through that again?' either gets you time or discourages the other party from using such complication. Sometimes, of course, it is not a ploy, it is an essential where the other party is trying to bundle separate elements together and you need to unpick them and consider them individually.

Onus transfer. Put the onus on the other party to come up with ideas, e.g. 'What must we do to enable you to reduce your price?' Sellers try to get the buyer's 'shopping list'. They then negotiate each item on the list in turn, finally asking for the order because they have agreed everything on the list.

Onus transfer enables the buyer to get the seller's shopping list, i.e. what the seller needs to drop prices. The buyer can then negotiate in the same way to arrive at the price he requires.

More generally, asking the other party to come up with ideas and suggestions is a very good way both of gleaning information and of making them feel personally valued. As ever, we are looking for personal warmth (we value their opinions) and professional toughness (we require some useful input that will meet our objectives).

Section C: Managing the Negotiation

Backburner. You can put off either to another meeting or to a later stage in the negotiation an item or issue that you had not planned for, giving yourself time to work out a position on the issue. This can sometimes result in the other party repeating all or part of their case and a comparison of first and second versions can prove useful.

This tactic can also be used where it appears that a particular issue is bogging down the negotiation. Proposing 'let's leave that for the moment' can prevent this happening. As the negotiation proceeds, the contentious issue often resolves itself and there is no need to revisit it.

Negotiating backwards. It can be helpful to try to find out in advance where the other person would like to end up. This can avoid the resentment that could occur when you push someone beyond what they see as their limit.

The hypothetical question: 'what if …' or 'suppose …'. This can be particularly useful for tabling a new idea or to help break deadlock. Matters can be discussed without the fear of commitment. The hypothetical question can, however, be a two-edged sword, depending on where it is used in a negotiation. If used during the exploratory/testing stage it can open up useful alternatives and help to shape a deal. If used late in the process, when the basic framework of a deal has been constructed, it can cause frustration since one or other party may see it as a backward rather than a forward step, breaking the framework and implying that the process has to start again.

Taking the temperature. An informal meeting or contact can be used to test for views, positions, sensitivities, etc. Be careful to define the purpose of such a meeting; do not reach a formal settlement informally. As always, be wary of informal emails and phone conversations that may result in an unintended verbal contract.

Divide and rule. Use this tactic when in a negotiation you are facing a team of negotiators on the other side. By listening and observing you may pick up more positive or agreeable signals from a particular member. You can then concentrate on them as being more reasonable and supportive. Sometimes the team actually begins to argue among themselves, so listen carefully for useful signals.

If leading a team negotiation, make certain during the preparation that steps are taken to ensure you do not fall into this trap.

New faces. Change to another team or refer to other individuals or groups. New faces need not be tied by what has been developed in the negotiation to date. This is a tactic often used overseas in international negotiations, and can be hugely frustrating if you are on the receiving end, since all the effort you have put in to establishing a personal rapport appears to be wasted. (Of course, that is one reason for deploying the tactic: nobody wants their own team to start 'going native'.) It is a good disruptor; it can allow a negotiation that has hit an impasse to scroll back to an earlier

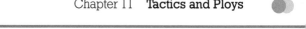

position and take a new course without loss of face, but it also eats time, and allows the opposition to see if your case second time around actually matches your initial position.

Section D: Tricks of the Trade

Here you will find not so much tactics and ploys, but observations on behaviours that you might use, or that you might recognize others using against you. As always, only use these where you are comfortable, where they may gain you an advantage, and when they go with, not against, the tactics and plans that you are deploying. (For example, 'Desperate Dan' cautions you against looking too eager, but if you really are facing a crisis – perhaps your usual supplier has gone bankrupt – there is no advantage in being overly coy about it; your potential new supplier does in this case need to know that your requirement is, at least, urgent, even if not quite 'desperate'.)

Use them at your discretion, but above all be aware of when they are being used on you!

Desperate Dan. Never look or sound too eager. It leads the other party to think that you need them more than they need you.

Sitting where? Pay attention to where people sit in the room. Let them sit down first and then position yourself near (or directly opposite) the decision maker. If you wish them to sit where you prefer then you could use nameplates. You may feel that, if you are effectively chairing the meeting, you should sit at the head of the table; but in practice, you can see a lot less of people's facial and other expressions from there, and in a negotiation between teams, there may be little chance of understanding any activity that seems to be going on at the foot of the table.

I'm busy but … Remember that your diary is always full of important meetings. You may be able to fit them in for a negotiation if you do a bit of juggling. Never have an empty diary (even if it is): you are a busy person, your time is precious, your views are in demand, and you are sufficiently engaged in the higher direction of the business not to have many clear slots. That at least is the impression you are trying to convey.

Dear John. Never forget the power of a mail merge. Keep all mail shots personal, and if you can disable the 'reply all' key on your email, do so.

Senior executive. If you have a junior-sounding job title do not put it on your business card: just your department will do. Conversely, if you are the boss do not let them know. Skilled negotiators are always pleased to see the boss: once the boss has agreed, who can stop the deal? Often, people have alternative job titles, depending on their audience. Phrases like VP or Director need to be considered in context: is this board level at the holding company or main group, or are they merely a big fish in a small, satellite operation? (But even if it is the latter, that does not necessarily mean that they lack the authority to sign off on the deal, it is just that you need to know.)

Personal history. Keep a keen interest in the other party's personal history. Use it wherever possible. Information is power. Salespeople often do this, buyers rarely do so.

Well-known phrase or saying. Check to see whether the other side have any habits or customs worth remembering. Listen to their words. Do they have any favourite expressions you could use back to them? Expressing things in the same style of language builds rapport, for example someone frequently using 'I see what you mean' could be someone who tends to think pictorially. Replay with 'Let me show you how my proposal would look'. If you are dealing frequently with someone, you may be able to spot characteristic mannerisms that suggest anxiety, or a need to buy thinking time: before workplace smoking bans came into force, pipe-smokers had a massive armoury of time-buying tactics available. Cleaning spectacles or snaffling the last digestive (because it is rude to talk with your mouth full) can also be ways of buying thinking time.

Clean and tidy. Your personal hygiene and dress tell much about you. Never be caught out in this area. 'Designer stubble' does not work in all situations. In the economic downturn at the time of writing, we are told that ties and more formal dress are back in, at least for male executives. Halitosis, BO (or smelling of the lunchtime pint) may be problematic. If your meeting room has been used by others recently it is important to check that it is free of lingering body odours, half-eaten chicken masala and generally stale air.

Shake hands. A poor handshake can cost you hundreds of pounds. Practise a good firm grip if necessary. Other countries have other habits: take advice on bowing and exchanging cards, in Japan, for example. Even in Latin countries, kissing on a first business date is probably not appropriate. Do not assume that you are on Christian or forename terms unless you have been invited to be so (and in parts of the East, be aware that the forename in our sense is not necessarily the one that comes first).

Shared experiences. Try to find at least two things that you and the other party have in common. Once discovered mention them regularly in conversation but do not overdo it, and do not 'fake' shared experiences or enthusiasms. If you cannot tell the difference

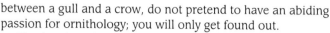

between a gull and a crow, do not pretend to have an abiding passion for ornithology; you will only get found out.

Closing in. When you are selling be careful with closed questions. Try some alternatives.

Fifteen all! You can always answer a question with a question. 'How can you lower your prices?' can be countered by 'How important is price to you compared with quality, let's say?'

It's good isn't it? Use question tags. 'This is quite a new development, Mr Smith, isn't it?' As you say 'isn't it' look the other party in the eyes and nod your head. They will be drawn in by your behaviour to agree with you, and indeed to go on to expand on the subject, which will be to your advantage in terms of gaining information. 'Yes, we're really excited about this, we've committed a lot', tells you quite a bit about the strength of your negotiating position.

Silence is golden. When you have asked a powerful question always be quiet and give the other party time to reply. Silence is an important issue. Do not fill it with your own words or be embarrassed by its use.

Rubber ball. If you feel you are being manipulated in a conversation then reverse the roles. Bounce it straight back with 'That's a good point. What do you think about it? I'm not too sure, myself'.

Evidence for the prosecution. Do not be impressed by computer printouts, statistics, thick documents, PowerPoint presentations and the like. They can all be easily manipulated. (However, be alert to the possibility that your opposite number may not be totally master of all this information. If you are presented with a complex case and you suspect you've got the equivalent of the office junior presenting it, the opportunities are considerable; although remembering that the objective is not to make him or her feel personally useless, it is to suggest that the higher powers they work for have in some sense let him or her down, that he or she is on their own, possibly even that only you can really help them understand the brief they have been given.)

Excuse me. If you feel that the other side is about to make a telling point interrupt and get your retaliation in first. It can deflate their advantage.

Nice and nasty. Do not be taken in by the Mr Nice and Mr Nasty performance. One character may give you a hard time while his colleague 'can do you a favour'. It is a well-rehearsed routine.

The hurry-up. Do not let the salesperson give you 'standing room only'. If you are told that there is only one in stock, that the offer will only last until the end of the week, just hang fire. Deals done in haste are often regretted.

Thank you for the furry dice. Even if you are offered something in a bargain that you don't want, never refuse it. You may be able to trade it back later for something that you do want.

Do not blink first. The side that suggests a compromise first may well be the weakest. Avoid it yourself and go for broke when it is suggested to you. (How about 99:1 as a suitable compromise?)

Confusion. Be well prepared and at the right moment throw a large number of variables onto the table: 'If you can give me the extra volume with the free delivery then I might be able to give you the payment terms you want, but only if you can package it for me.' This complication can confuse the poorly prepared. If it happens to you call a timeout immediately or admit that it is complicated and ask for a recap.

Something for nothing. Always have available one or two things that will cost you nothing which you could give as a sign of goodwill or, better still, trade for something valuable.

Let me have a word with them. When the other party uses a lever against you, destroy it immediately. Policy can be changed, offer to help them write to the bank manager, offer to speak to their boss. 'This is clearly difficult for you, but we may be able to help – let me have a word with your MD/bank/suppliers' (of parts or of finance). If the constraint is not genuine they will have to modify their position; if it is genuine, you may as a potential buyer be in a position to influence things to mutual advantage.

Call my bluff. Do not buckle when faced with an ultimatum. It is probably true that they need this deal as much as you. Do not be afraid to hear tough words at this stage and wade through them. Ask yourself if they would really walk away. Remember that if they ever move on a 'final' offer then their credibility will be seriously diminished.

Let's shake. Put your hand across the table when you wish to close the deal. The other party will then have to refuse to shake if they want to continue negotiating.

Let me finish. Do not allow yourself to be interrupted when you wish to make a key point. It is easy to have your point devalued with a trivial interruption concerning the heating or draught from a window, or a query on your use of a particular term that is not actually germane to what you are trying to say. Spurious interruptions are often a sign that people are getting tired and unfocused. Do not let this stop you making your point, but you could consider it as a sign to call a comfort break.

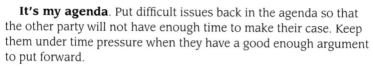

It's my agenda. Put difficult issues back in the agenda so that the other party will not have enough time to make their case. Keep them under time pressure when they have a good enough argument to put forward.

Questions answered with questions. If you are asked a tough question reply with 'That's an interesting point, Mr Wilkinson. What prompts you to ask that?' You may just be able to sidetrack him from making a significant point and allow yourself some breathing space while he answers questions from you.

You know what I mean. Let the other party interpret your words in their own way. It is their prerogative.

Last chance and final offers. Try to get the other party to move from a 'final' offer. It will be a good opportunity for you to test their skill and experience.

I beg your pardon. Do not be afraid to interrupt immediately if the other party seems to have made a verbal error, especially one in their favour. Again, having the notes to back you up is vital.

Do we or don't we? Check the negatives in the terms and conditions. Unscrupulous negotiators can easily omit a 'not' or change a date.

I'm in charge. Do not be put off by power handshakes and aggressive behaviour. Most of this is a sham designed to put you on the defensive.

Let me ask you a question. If you find the other person leading you with a battery of questions break the sequence. Do not allow yourself to be taken on the 'yes, you're right' path.

Let's be friends. Make a conscious effort to create rapport with the other party. Follow their words and gestures and try to agree with what they are saying as far as is professionally permissible, but beware of the sort of subconscious imitation, especially of accents, that could be construed as offensive, and of being drawn into the sort of (typically but not exclusively male) banter that may be offensive to others present.

I'm not sure that I agree. 'Yes, but' is more powerful than 'No'.

Do you really like me? Be careful if you find the other party agreeing with you too readily. What do they *really* think?

It's only a game. Some negotiators will purposely try to upset you so that you lose control for a moment or become sidetracked by your feelings. Remember that negotiation at this stage is only a game and you should treat it accordingly.

Group therapy. In team negotiations be careful of caucus discussions in the toilet or over lunch. You can be excluded from important ideas when separated into smaller groups. (See also my comments above about the risk of chairing from the head of the table: you may not be aware of side-deals being arranged at the other end of the polished mahogany.)

The non-commercial novice. Watch the engineers in your team. They are notoriously prone to giving away key points at crucial times. The technical members of the team must be as well trained as the commercial people when it comes to a team negotiation. (In fairness, this is not just about engineers; in many modern negotiations all sorts of functions from finance to human resources, if you are negotiating an outsourcing, for example, will legitimately be present and have their own agendas. But precisely because these are committed professionals, it is easy for them to emphasize their own concerns at the expense of the overall objectives.)

Time management. If the other side wishes to delay the flow with a ploy, leave the room. Being asked to sit idly while they make a call or crunch some numbers gives them the advantage. Use this as a chance to freshen up and collect your thoughts out of the room. (It is also courteous not to listen in to their private conversations with their headquarters.)

Walk this way. Be careful of the walk from reception up to the office. At this early, unguarded moment important information can be often unwittingly given away, often by a relatively junior member of staff. Having the latest graduate trainee explain how privileged she feels to be working in this dynamic organization where the sky's the limit is nice, but it is not helpful if you are about to plead poverty and ask for a price freeze.

Remember

1. Tactics need to be used with discretion.
2. What will work in a positive way with one person could equally be a negative with another.
3. Every negotiation is different and you will need to consider which tactics are appropriate.

12

Negotiating Across the Globe

'The past is a foreign country: they do things differently there'
(L.P. Hartley)

Introduction

In earlier chapters I refer to the approaches taken in different parts of the world and quote some real-life examples to assist understanding. I predominantly focus on the UK and USA and the reader will have been able to gain an insight into negotiating with those people from an American or Anglo background.

This chapter takes a broad look at negotiation in other parts of the world as well: the Far East, the Latin-speaking countries, North Africa/the Middle East, Central Europe and Scandinavia, and it also includes a section on culture cues in North America. It would be useful when the reader is studying these culture cues to compare with the comments from earlier chapters and develop a culture cue chart for Anglo-influenced negotiators.

This chapter also includes a section on belief, social, business, legal, financial and logistical systems. The questions that need to be addressed for each of these systems are included and the chapter finishes with a list of major errors in international negotiations.

One method of negotiating is bargaining: some people are said to 'drive a hard bargain'. Although the content of a bargain may be similar the world over, i.e. price, quantity, quality, and so on, the manner in which it is arrived at can change markedly depending on the country in which the 'driving' is being done.

Staying with the analogy of driving, if you use your own car and drive in another country you may be in the same driving seat but you could be driving on the other side of the road, which not only feels strange but makes manoeuvres such as overtaking more difficult. The signs and signals are different, as is the behaviour. In France *'priorité à droite'*, although not very common nowadays, allows as a norm behaviour that elsewhere would cause great annoyance to the driver on the main road, who would be screeching to a halt to make way for the car joining at speed from the side road on the right.

The point is that wherever you are in the world, while similar components are used to build a car, its safe and effective use depends on the driver adapting to the local environment.

So it is with a negotiation. My experience leads me to conclude that the five main styles of negotiation and the four main phases apply all over the world. What does change is a people's natural preference for one style over another. So in some countries you may see a preference for the use of logic, whereas others may prefer threat or emotion. Likewise in some countries you may detect a preference for bargaining or compromise. Although even with its severe limitations compromise is better than not negotiating at all, my personal research indicates that this is all too often the default mode in UK business.

Some negotiations do fail. Such failures are usually due to one or more of the following:

1 The views or positions of the parties involved are simply irreconcilable.

2 One party may be taken beyond their terms of reference or limits of authority and can go no further.

3 There may be severe clashes of personality or culture and one or other party simply refuses to deal. The grounds may be personal (for some reason you cannot build the required level of interpersonal trust with the other party), or there is an alien business culture or even legal framework that cannot be reconciled with the normal and accepted ways that you and your organization do business.

Observing some simple basic rules in international negotiations can minimize the effect of the last of these reasons.

This is not necessarily anything to do with racial or cultural prejudice as such, although it is sad but true that many such prejudgements are consciously or unconsciously maintained. Since one of the principal messages of this book is that the negotiator must always and constantly be testing and verifying the validity of any prior judgement he or she has made, even on merely technical issues, it should be clear that there is no place for prejudice in the interpersonal and cultural aspects of a negotiation either.

It is particularly important to remember this because in this chapter we are going to look at some stereotypes of negotiating behaviour in different cultures and countries. The point about stereotypes is that they *do* contain some degree of truth, but that is at best a statistical truth. It may be true that Japanese, or a man/woman, or a finance director, is more likely to behave in a particular way in a given circumstance, but it is by no means a certainty.

Bear in mind too that many organizations are profoundly cross-cultural, even global. The UK subsidiary of a Japanese company may have an American MD and the purchasing director may be French (but may have trained or worked in, say, Germany). Which particular stereotype of negotiating behaviour are you expecting? There may be no dominant culturally determined negotiating style; if there is you need to discover it with eyes and ears wide open, not merely assume that it is there.

To summarize: for you, as a guest overseas:

1 **The rules of the road will be different**. You may be dealing in a country where decisions are made by committee rather than by one individual in whom is vested total authority to negotiate and close the deal. In the former it may be that the real negotiation goes on behind the scenes within the committee during an adjournment: you are presented with a sequence of positions to which you must choose how to respond.

2 **The signals will be different**. The Russian's stony face may not signify lack of interest, but merely his personal concern not to appear too friendly or too ready to accept since he is unlikely to be permitted to do either.

3 **The behaviour will be different**. The Japanese 'yes' may mean 'no' … yes he understands, no he disagrees. The American's drive to win a deal as soon as possible will offend the Middle Eastern negotiator who needs time – and plenty of it – to measure you up as a worthy counterpart or otherwise. Bear in mind too that your counterparts will likewise be grappling with their own ideas or stereotypes, on greater or lesser validity, of how you are likely to behave.

Systems

Figure 12.1 illustrates a number of the influences that will affect you and your approach, and a checklist for each one follows. Use these lists as an aeroplane pilot uses checklists so that nothing is overlooked which may have serious consequences.

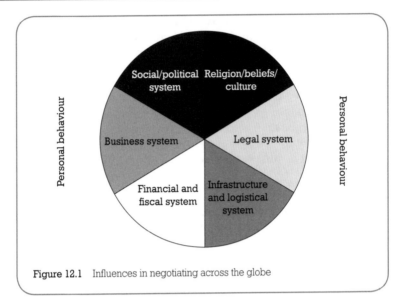

Figure 12.1   Influences in negotiating across the globe

The Social System – Key Questions

- What is the level of formality expected in terms of dress, use of first names, use of titles, etc.?

- Is business conducted only in the office or also after hours, e.g. over a drink or dinner or on a golf course?

- Do social meetings involve partners, families and home visits, or is all entertaining done in restaurants, clubs, etc.?

- What is expected or permitted in the way of gifts?

- Do people willingly accept criticism in front of others or only in private? How important are questions of honour or loss of face?

- Are there particular issues, e.g. matters of religion or politics or sex, which are openly discussed here, or which are taboo?

- Do women participate in business and, if so, is it on equal terms with men?

- What levels of tactility are permissible/normal within business?

The Business System – Key Questions

■ How is business conducted? Is it primarily between the principals of firms or are all levels involved? Is there any real delegation of authority? Can the apparent hierarchy be trusted?

■ Is everything expected to be put in writing or are verbal agreements treated as binding? What significance is given to contracts? If formal contracts are not treated as significant, then what, if anything replaces them?

■ Do professional advisors, e.g. lawyers, play a major role in negotiations and the decision-making process, or are they regarded as subordinates whose primary function is to 'get the words right'? What other advisors might contribute?

■ Are formal meetings conducted only between the leaders of both teams, with the other members only speaking if they are specifically asked to do so?

■ Is industrial espionage practised? How careful must one be to lock papers away or even not bring them at all?

■ Are inducements, sweeteners and baksheesh necessary to secure and/or carry out business? If so, how is it operated and what are the usual terms? Is this accepted and legal, or prevalent but nominally illegal? Even if it is legal 'over there' is it legal in your own home country? Is it contrary to your own organization's ethical code of practice?

■ Can contracts be negotiated with one firm or must they, by law or as a matter of practice, be put out to competitive bid? If the latter, what are usually the key criteria for securing the award? Is it just a matter of price (this may particularly apply to public sector contracts, as is the case in the EU countries)?

■ Do negotiations proceed in two stages, first the technical and then the commercial? Are negotiations conducted by levels, each of which will expect to obtain some concessions? Do the operational level people you are negotiating with have final authority? (In Germany, for example, there is often a 'supervisory board' typically including labour representation, which may have the final say on major contracts. In other countries, state organs may have similar powers of veto.)

■ In what language is business conducted? Can documents be in two languages, one of which is English, and both be of equal validity?

- Can contracts be amended verbally as well as in written format?
- Will negotiations be with an export/import agency, or direct with the operating company? Even if direct, there may be a purchasing department involved who can be expected to have different motives to the actual users. Again, there may be a political dimension, e.g. a requirement for part of the value of the contract to be offset to the local economy in one way or another.

Religion – Key Questions

- What is the predominant religion of the country with which you are negotiating? (Note that religion in this context is to be interpreted as including, for example, communism or other ruling or predominant philosophies and belief systems.)
- Does that religion influence significantly:
  - the conduct of political affairs
  - the legal system
  - the nature or country of origin of products that may be purchased (an obvious example would be embargoes in some Muslim states against Israeli products)
  - social relations and individual behaviour
  - the entry of personnel having particular nationalities or other religious beliefs or political affiliations
  - the incidence of holidays and working hours, e.g. Ramadan?

The Political System – Key Questions

Determine the extent of state control of business enterprises.

- If state control exists:
  - Is it organized centrally or regionally?
  - What are the limits of devolved authority from the centre?
  - With which state authority/enterprise must the negotiations take place, i.e. is there more than one, and if so, what are their interrelationships? (This can be very complex, even in Western countries, as anyone who has tried to buy or develop property in Spain may know to their cost.)
- What is the extent of political interest in the particular project?
  - Who is interested?
  - What are the respective powers of those who are interested?

- What is the stability of the present regime? Is it likely to change in the lifetime of the project? When are elections scheduled to take place and is the project in question an election issue?

- What are the political relations between the governments of the seller and purchaser?
  - How susceptible are these to the acts of the other (e.g. the showing of the film *The Death of a Princess* or human rights activism)?
  - Are these relations likely to change if there is a change in the political persuasion of the government of either country?

The Legal System – Key Questions

- What is the legal system? Is it codified (e.g. on the 'Napoleonic' model that applies across much of Europe) or derived from English (or other, e.g. Swiss) common law?

- Is it mandatory, and enforceable, to accept that the contract must be governed by the purchaser's legal system? (You would probably want the contract to be adjudicable by your own system and courts if possible.)

- What is the level of enforcement of laws and regulations in practice? What are your chances of redress if something goes wrong? What liabilities may you as a buyer incur if your supplier either defaults or breaks local law apparently on your behalf?

- To what extent are the courts and the judiciary independent of the executive?

- To what extent are the courts and judiciary biased in favour of a 'domestic' actor within a contract?

- What level of influence in practice could the purchaser or a major subcontractor or another counter-party exercise over the judiciary?

- What is the timescale for court proceedings?

- What means exist for the enforcement of court judgments?

- Is there any procedure, and if so what, for the enforcement of foreign judgments/arbitration awards?

- What is the typical arbitration process used in the event of dispute?

- Is the purchaser's legal system such as to:
  - inhibit his negotiations in making arrangements, making concessions, etc.
  - restrict the authority of those able to conclude, award or amend contracts to specified officers of the purchaser's corporation?

- Are there reliable local firms of lawyers independent of the purchaser and of other interested parties?

- Is it necessary legally to establish a local company to carry out local work? If so, what are the rules in particular on the proportions of overseas to local shareholding, fees for management services and remittance of profits?

- What are the relevant laws on employment and social security? How are those applied to non-nationals? Is there a required ratio of local non-national employees? Must an engineer be employed who is a member of the local engineering institute? These may differ as you establish a locally registered company as opposed to operating, if this is permitted, as a foreign company. Is there a formal Mutual Recognition of Qualifications (MRQ), and does this work in practice? (Across the EU, MRQ exists in a number of professions, but professionals may still find themselves unrecognized as such by courts and tribunals.)

The Financial and Fiscal System – Key Questions

- What is the financial rating of the area concerned? (This may be vastly different from the rating of the individual company you are dealing with.)

- What is the country's debt service ratio? Has the country applied to the International Monetary Fund for assistance and, if so, with what results?

- How large are the country's overseas exchange reserves? On what commodities does it primarily depend for overseas earnings?

- Is the country's currency freely exchangeable? If not, what are the restrictions?

- What is the country's record on honouring payment obligations, and are delays likely?

- Can you obtain Letters of Credit confirmed in London?

- What procedures have to be gone through with the central bank or Ministry of Finance for obtaining payments in foreign currencies?

- What are the applicable tax taws? In particular, on what does the liability for tax depend? Can tax be limited to work performed in the country concerned? Are there any double taxation conventions in force and, if so, with which countries?

- Is the remittance of the final payment subject to the issue of a tax clearance certificate? If so, how is this obtained and how long does it take?

- Can profits earned by a local company be remitted overseas? If so, what are the rules and procedures?

- What are the regulations on the payment of customs duties? Can the contract be exempt from duty?

- Are there any fees such as stamp duties, taxes or invoices which the contractor will have to pay?

The Infrastructure and Logistical System – Key Questions

- What is the local availability of:
    - required labour, both skilled and unskilled
    - professional staff
    - materials for construction
    - constructional plant
    - maintenance facilities
    - competent and financially sound subcontractors?

- What restrictions are there on:
    - importation of staff and labour
    - importation of materials which are made locally
    - importation of plant?

- In which language will the contract be negotiated and administered? What is the availability of business-competent and secure translators?

- What are the local logistical problems relating to port unloading facilities and waiting time, dockside and hinterland storage facilities, and road, rail or air infrastructure to and from ports? If you need to position your own people in-country for the duration of the contract, are there suitable hotels or other property? Less of a problem in the 'mobile' age, but do the telephones work?

Personal Behaviour

You, as a guest overseas, have three roles when negotiating:

- as an observer
- as an individual participant in the environment
- as a negotiator.

Do	Do not
1. Be sensitive to the local social, business and religious customs	1. Go native
2. Be aware of the local political scene and how it may affect both your project happening and your chances of success	2. Involve yourself in any form of political activity or express publicly your opinion on political affairs
3. Behave courteously and be respectful to ministers and officials	3. Be subservient or allow yourself to be intimidated or overawed by their status or by the shock tactics they may use to impress upon you their superiority or power
4. Prepare yourself in advance for all meetings and stay calm	4. Be surprised at the unexpected or allow yourself to get flustered
5. Take every opportunity to get out and about and talk to people	5. Succumb to local temptation
6. Have as team members those whose personality and technical abilities are likely to fit in with those with whom negotiations will be conducted	6. Allow your expertise, however brilliant, to patronize the client or try to teach him his business
7. Be flexible and willing to adjust to their conceptions provided you can still obtain your objectives even if the means are different	7. Be rigid and insist that yours is the only way

8. Be careful of security of your papers and discreet in referring to people, particularly your contacts, by name	8. Be eager to show off your limited knowledge
9. Listen to your agent's advice with an open mind	9. Try to teach him his business or impose your preconceived ideas
10. Be patient	10. Leave the territory unguarded at critical stages even if you miss a board meeting or your holiday

Figure 12.2 Personal behaviour dos and don'ts

Cultural Cues

There follow some notes on some of the characteristic behaviours you may encounter when negotiating with individuals and companies from around the world. But do remember all that I said earlier about the dangers of stereotypes. Every individual you meet is just that: an individual. However much they may appear at first glance to conform to national or cultural stereotypes, they may have quite different and surprising behaviours and motivations. Your 'typical' Japanese or Indian may have an MBA from Harvard or Oxford. Conversely, they may be expecting you to be stereotypical of your country: how upset would you be as a Scot or a Yorkshireman or an East Ender if your negotiating counter-party insists on treating you as an incarnation of Hugh Grant?

There are other considerations. Firstly, it is very likely that the individuals, companies or organizations you are dealing with around the world have already attracted themselves to you precisely because they appear to buck the trend: they seem to be more like 'Western' companies than the rest. This may be true, or it may be a PR slick or spin.

Secondly, and contrarily, this book is being completed at the height of a credit crunch, which may have temporarily discredited the supposed Anglo-Saxon model of free-market capitalism. That in itself will not change the fundamental negotiating styles of the individuals you deal with (unless they have read this book and practised new techniques!); it does, however, mean that in many cultures and societies the corporate/organizational behaviour (and thus the objectives of negotiations) may shift back to a more corporate/

statist and probably risk-averse mode. This may make the problem of distinguishing the negotiating styles of individuals, and the negotiation agendas of their organizations, even more problematic.

These notes give some indication of behaviours you may expect to find in the following parts of the world (… but your expectations may be very wrong!):

- the Far East

- the Latin-speaking countries

- North Africa and the Middle East

- Central Europe

- Scandinavia

- North America.

I would also strongly recommend reading *Riding the Waves of Culture* (Trompenaars and Hampden-Turner, 1997) and *Culture's Consequences* (Hofstede, 2001).

Negotiation Cues for the Far East

Behavioural characteristics	Methods of persuasion	Key needs	Key tactics
Formal	Logic	Save face	Commitment
Polite	Discreet use of power	Entrance to market	Time delays
Thorough		Volume	High offers
Efficient		Long preliminaries	Package deal
Always in a group		Long-term relationship	Silence
High-tech			
Long-term view			
Nothing is ever final		Preserve harmony	Revisiting old issues
Pragmatic approach to rules, regulations and small print		Respect for authority and hierarchy	Never reveal their full hand

Some Dos

- Remember they look for long-term relationships: allow time for personal relationships to develop.

- Remember, they try to work towards a *perceived* win/win result.

- Look closely at proposals: they look for a *perceived* win/win situation and are not above some slight deception to achieve this – beware of the unexpected.

- Be prepared for rapid movement once a deal is agreed.

- Use negotiators at the appropriate status level, corresponding to theirs. Remember that status is based more on age and experience than titles.

- Remember, they take a more long-term view than Western negotiators. They tend towards aggressive pricing policies and market penetration – they aim to maximize sales rather than profits. Profits will then follow.

- Be prepared to give as much information as possible about you, your company and your product/service. It might look like an interrogation but they expect this to be provided.

- Be prepared for renegotiation if circumstances change significantly. Deals/agreements are reached on the basis of circumstances pertaining at the time; if these change, then renegotiation will be seen as being in order.

- Have full appropriate information, plenty of time and belief in your case – *they will have*!

LISTEN for signals – they will often hint obliquely rather than make specific demands or give a firm 'no'.

Remember, the exchange of small gifts is seen as no more than politeness.

Some Don'ts

- Do not expect to receive the full story if you push for markers or information early on in discussions.

- Do not try to 'divide and rule': their emphasis is on the consensus – the group as a whole must agree.

- Do not try and rush them: there needs to be time for all members of their team to be consulted. It may be necessary to consult others who are not actually present, e.g. production for shorter lead times. Only when all parties in any way involved have been consulted will a decision be given.

■ Do not be arrogant or aggressive: they often attribute these characteristics to Westerners.

■ Do not take an absence of 'No' to indicate agreement: they do not like to say 'No' as this is considered impolite.

■ Do not be put off by long silences; they are not embarrassed by these.

■ Do not overdo the legal documentation to back an agreement as this could be construed as a lack of trust.

■ Do not use this as an opportunity to flex your corporate muscles if you work for a large organization.

■ Do not force them into a situation where they could be seen to have failed. Never make them lose face. (That is actually a good principle in any situation.)

For further reading refer to CRC, M. Yoshimori (Japan), *Doing Business in Japan*.

Negotiation Cues for the Latin-Speaking Countries

Behavioural characteristics	Methods of persuasion	Key needs	Key tactics
Proud	Emotion	Respect – personal and professional for their country	Delays
Emotional	Bargaining	Enthusiasm	Intelligent debate
Nationalistic		Animated conversation	Relationships
Family oriented		Flair	Play hard to get
Cultured		Honour	
Lively		Creativity	
Intellectual			Demonstrative, but often empty, emotional displays

Some Dos

- Show respect for their country and culture, e.g. try to speak their language, learn something about their traditions, in particular family traditions, food, wine, etc.

- Respect their formality, in both business and personal relationships, e.g. do try to get a personal introduction.

- Be clear, concise and logical: demonstrate through preparation.

- Be prepared to argue your case: a good debate is often enjoyed.

- Show interest in the *person* but do not pry into personal areas; keep it general.

- Remember, they base their case on experience – the actual situation – and pre-established criteria. Concept is important to them.

- Be prepared to haggle and bargain: know what concession will cost you.

- Be prepared for more than just an agreement in principle as once an agreement has been reached, their sense of honour means this must be kept and vice versa.

- Be honest: you will go up in their estimation as it will appeal to their sense of honour.

- Demonstrate how, once an agreement has been reached, schedules and deadlines will be met.

Some Don'ts

- Do not try to exploit personal relationships for business purposes: keep them separate.

- Do not put either yourself or the client under pressure for a decision or rush an agreement. This may well be concluded over a meal; remember, the ritual of dining/eating is a very important aspect of their culture, and this applies equally to both business and pleasure.

- Do not make adverse comments about any of their customs or traditions.

- Do not try to be too clever: this could be seen as being devious.

- Do not be surprised if they appear initially to stick rigidly to their position. Their preparation has probably convinced them that their case is the only 'right' one. Hear it out and then *persuade* rather than just disagree.

Negotiation Cues for North Africa and the Middle East

Behavioural characteristics	Methods of persuasion	Key needs	Key tactics
Very polite	Bargaining	Respect	'One more thing'
Persistent and they don't forget	Threat, implied, that appears particularly over the long term	Time to build a relationship	Time – under no pressure
Unhurried		Understanding their culture/religion	Courtesy
Hospitable		Avoid negatives	'Open' – very high but enjoy bargaining
Well prepared			

Some Dos

■ Remember they have a very strong tradition of hospitality: be prepared for this to take time but it should not be construed as inducement or an indication of progress.

■ Allow time to build a relationship: this also reflects a need to establish a climate of trust prior to the actual negotiation.

■ Be prepared to adapt to cultural differences, especially as regards time.

■ Remember, the Arabs to a great extent are one large family: your problem is that you do not belong! The Muslim religion is predominant so try to acquire some knowledge about Islam and its history. As in most cultures other than the Anglo-Saxon, nepotism is seen as a virtue rather than a vice: it is their family duty to recommend their second cousin as a subcontractor, and given the strength of family ties and honour this may actually be your best guarantee of a job well done.

■ Always remain courteous.

■ Remember that bargaining is a way of life – and enjoyed. An opening offer may appear ridiculous but never say so; they will eventually move from this position.

■ Be prepared for the 'just one more thing' tactic.

■ Match their persistence: they enjoy a good debate.

- Be prepared: they spend much time preparing their case.

- *Listen*: their politeness prevents them making direct requests; they hint rather than ask outright.

- Be prepared for interruptions: their innate hospitality must be offered to all visitors even if it is not really convenient.

Some Don'ts
- Do not overdo eye contact: this can be resented.

- Do not use time-pressure tactics, and if they are used on you, avoid any overreaction. You are probably being tested to see how you react.

- Do not use direct negative statements: be diplomatic when saying 'No'.

- Do not be surprised if, after agreement is reached, modifications to the agreement are requested should circumstances change: everything, including the future, belongs to God.

- Never use any form of behaviour that could be construed as patronizing.

- As a general rule, do not try to do business without an Arab agent.

- For more information refer to CRC negotiations seminar M. Mezouar (Morocco), *Doing Business on the Arabian Peninsula*.

Negotiation Cues for Central Europe

(Not including Scandinavia or the Latin Mediterranean countries)

Behavioural characteristics	Methods of persuasion	Key needs	Key tactics
Logical	Logic/threat	Honour	Conservative presentation
Formal	Compromise	Quality	Analysis
Polite	Bargaining	Professional	Modest concessions
Meticulous		Reliability	Linguistics
Efficient		Respect	Unmoving
Nationalistic		Privacy preserved	Mild deception
Fair			Apparent refusal to comprehend the opponent's decision
Verbally indirect			
Appear inflexible			

Some Dos

■ Be punctual: they are!

■ Remember, they place store on quality and expect a negotiating team to have experts who can answer detailed questions on this point.

■ They are often clear about what they want and can be tough and ruthless.

■ Prepare well and thoroughly: they do, and will not respect others who do not.

■ Observe the ritual of introduction.

■ If they are visiting you, remember they enjoy pleasant and comfortable surroundings: try to establish a relaxed relationship.

■ Spend time on building rapport.

■ Listen carefully as they can be devious: language can be used to wrap up key information and they often understate matters to avoid exaggeration.

- Persuade rather than challenge, remembering that *logic* has great appeal.

- Try to stick with predetermined plans: problems can arise if they are forced to deal with other subjects of which they have had no notice.

- Remember, compromise can be a good ploy: they tend to see this as settling at a halfway point, which may give more than you thought possible.

- Be prepared to debate issues, even though this is not really negotiation.

- Demonstrate a commitment to constant product/process development.

- Be prepared to *demonstrate* quality.

- Be prepared to work long and unsociable hours in pursuit of agreement.

- Dress appropriately: they tend to be formal, although a dark suit is perfectly safe.

- They appear to have a superior and persistent attitude, which can be disconcerting: defend your position and persevere.

One Don't
- Do not use too much emotion or be overfamiliar: they find this embarrassing.

Negotiation Cues for Scandinavia

Behavioural characteristics	Methods of persuasion	Key needs	Key tactics
Reserved	Logic/threat	Reliability	Logic
Quiet	Compromise	Evidence	Enthusiasm
Serious		Trust; want a complete professional proposal	Novelty
Self-critical			Facts and figures
Trustworthy			Push hard for opponent to reveal full goals and motives
Interested in new ideas			
Regard for quality			
Nationalistic and superior at times			

Some Dos

■ Study the history and achievements of the particular country you are visiting: their histories are different and demonstrating an interest will stand you in good stead. (This applies to any area, for example South-East Asia, that we may tend to think of as a homogeneous entity but which in reality comprises many different countries and cultures.)

■ Act with quietness and restraint: give them time to get to know you and form an impression of your country.

■ Be well informed about current affairs and the product or service you are offering: they pride themselves on this.

■ Have your proposal and information clearly and logically set out: be prepared to support argument with easily understood facts and figures.

■ Be enthusiastic: believe in what you are offering.

■ Try to learn a few phrases in their language: they will appreciate this, although they generally expect to do business in English.

- Remember to thank where appropriate: better to be a little overpolite than to offend by omission.

Some Don'ts

- Do not think of the whole of Scandinavia as being the same. There are similarities, but be aware of the differences.

- Do not try to rush them. Make time to ensure this does not occur. Agreement takes time.

- Do not bluff: be in command of relevant facts and admit a lack of knowledge if you do not know something.

- Do not be overfamiliar: let them make the first running.

- *Do not* attempt to drink and drive: driving after consuming any alcohol is a serious offence.

Negotiation Cues for North America

Behavioural characteristics	Methods of persuasion	Key needs	Key tactics
Enthusiastic	Bargaining	To win	Time pressure
Tough	Power/threat. Size/power can mean you have a hammer, and all you can see are nails!	Best deal	Speed/action
Persistent		Recognition	Bit by bit
Stubborn		Bottom line	
Action-oriented		Business	
Competitive		Action	Use of corporate name and muscle to intimidate
Friendly			
Superficial			Packaging/ bundling and unpackaging the deal
Patriotic			
Impatient			
Isolationist			

Some Dos

- Prepare well: they usually do, in terms of what they want and are prepared to give.

- Be prepared for an adversarial approach, often involving what we may think is strong language. They argue in a confrontational way: it is not usually personal!

- Try to find out their fall-back position: they usually prepare one. It is often possible to push them to this point in return for a relatively minor concession.

- Winning is important: allow them to *think* they have won – they expect to! They may then be generous in 'victory'.

- Be prepared to be creative: put ideas forward. 'What if' is to be encouraged.

- Use *all* methods of persuasion: North Americans tend to concentrate on bargaining, sometimes with threat.

- Read any paperwork carefully: they can be very quick to go to law if even minor breaches occur.

- Try and leave room in your proposals for discounts, special offers or similar: these go down well.

Some Don'ts

- Do not allow yourself to be overwhelmed by argument: soak it up and *listen*.

- Do not lose sight of your overall goal: Americans often negotiate via a series of small conflicts which can obscure the overall objective.

- Do not be ambiguous: keep things clear and simple.

- Do not yield to time pressures: 'deadline' is often used as a tactic.

- Do not be railroaded into a rushed deal: insist on time to read the small print of any paperwork/contract carefully and put this time to good use.

- Do not neglect testimonials from other users/contacts: they expect these and set great store by them. Why should they deal with you?

- Do not be intimidated by shows of corporate strength and power or ostentatious facilities.

Major Errors in International Negotiations

(Derived from Fayerweather and Kapoor, 1976)

1 Failure to place yourself in the other person's shoes:
Understand his position but still more, his reasons (the cultural sticks and carrots).

2 Insufficient understanding of different ways of thinking and the role of personal relations and personalities:
What is the thought process? Logical, factual, intuitive, impressionistic, imaginative? The relative importance of personal relationships is not the same in all cultures.

3 Insufficient knowledge of the host country:
History, culture, role of government, status of business, views on overseas visitors, etc.

4 Insufficient attention to saving face of the opponent:
Personal honour is a very sensitive issue in certain cultures.

5 Insufficient recognition of political/other criteria:
Political considerations, competition, both national and foreign.

6 Insufficient recognition of the decision-making process:
Several layers of decision makers, local authorities, interdepartmental conflicts.

7 Insufficient allocation of time for negotiations:
Distance, complexity of decision-making process, mutual suspicion, different attitudes towards time – again cultural differences of which you need to be aware.

8 Insufficient attention to planning, to internal communications and procedures:
Including interference by head offices.

9 Insufficient attention to the two-fold role of the negotiator:
To defend his position and to reach for agreement. A reliance upon preconceived assumptions and prejudices.

13

Practical Cases and Dilemmas: Testing Your Knowledge

We have had a lot of theory in the previous chapters; it seems time to apply some of this to some real-life situations. Some of these draw on typical business experiences, while others are based on negotiations you may have as a private citizen but, as I hope is already clear, the principles are the same.

What follows is a set of typical negotiating scenarios. Scenarios 1–18 have multiple-choice answers and scenarios 19–29 do not, but I would encourage you to develop alternative answers before turning to the solutions in the text. If the particular scenario seems a little divorced from your concerns, you could try translating it into some equivalent situation closer to home. This will allow you to develop a broader thinking in relation to negotiation and prepare you to deal with practical situations. You should gain some understanding of how you are likely to react in particular circumstances, and whether that is likely to be the best reaction possible.

Work through these scenarios and make a note of your views. After each scenario you will find my analysis and points together with, in some cases, the best course of action. You can refer back to these when faced with similar situations in the future: try the option suggested and see if you get better results! There are no prizes; no absolute right answers. Your own responses in, for example, a scenario involving a car or a house, will already be conditioned by any previous experience of buying (or selling) a car or a house. But that is all to the good. Think about what those prior experiences mean: how might they be influencing your behaviour in another, totally unrelated, negotiation? Would you, for example, negotiate to buy a second-hand machine-tool for your company in the same way that you would negotiate to buy a second-hand car for your teenager? And if not, why not?

Scenario 30 gives a detailed review of a supply and industrial relations problem experienced by a major airline. I have included it because it is a perfect example of an inappropriate negotiation stance being adopted.

Scenario 1

You are a sales manager and you have been told by your management that it is necessary to achieve an average 20 per cent price increase on all sales in order to counteract currency exchange rates which have moved sharply against you. If you cannot achieve this, or close to it, your company will have to cease trading. The current inflation rate is 3–4 per cent per annum and most customers, if they needed to, could buy elsewhere within three or four months.
  Would you:

(a) Ring up the buyers within your major customers and ask for a price increase?

(b) Send a letter to your customers requesting a price increase?

(c) Request a meeting with the buyers without specifying the reason'?

(d) Invite them to lunch (or whatever other hospitality your firm's ethical code allows) and then outline the problem but focusing only on currency, leaving any discussion of a price increase until later?

(e) Do something else?

Answer

Option (d) is preferred. Negotiation can begin sooner than you may think. Refer back to the illustration 'Devaluation' in Chapter 4. You outline the problem over lunch, but do not ask for a price increase at that time: this is a seed-sowing exercise designed to condition the buyer to expect a price increase at some time in the future. Alternatively, you could begin the conditioning on the telephone, but similarly sowing the conditioning seed rather than putting your marker straight down.

  If we think about life's experiences in general there are many times when our behaviour has been conditioned in simple ways. For example, static electric shocks in hotel lifts or from cars can make us wary when we hold handles or press buttons; but there are more pleasant forms of conditioning as well. Hospitality, in the broadest sense and even if it involves trivial expenditure, is extremely effective: most human beings seem to be hard wired to want to reciprocate in some way: it bonds people in the same way that apes bond by grooming each other. (Obviously, the reciprocation you are looking for is not another lunch, it's a better deal!)

Scenario 2

You have asked the buyer of a regular customer for a price increase of 4.8 per cent on a normal item. Current inflation is running at 5 per cent per annum.

What is the most effective remark that the buyer can now make and what is the best remark from a seller's point of view?

(a) 'No.'

(b) 'Why?'

(c) 'I was thinking of a decrease resulting from efficiencies brought about by productivity improvements.'

(d) 'I can only afford half.'

(e) 'Can it be delayed?'

Answer

For the buyer, the best remark is (c). This clearly indicates that getting the increase will not be easy and this may reduce the seller's expectations.

For the seller, (e) is the best alternative. This indicates that the buyer is probably prepared to pay since all that is asked for is delay. The way the question is put is very tentative and any objections can be overcome.

Option (b) could be very dangerous for a buyer. If 'why' is asked and a logical explanation is given, the buyer will be forced back on the defensive (see Chapter 7). It is very important to note that the opening statement by the buyer here can predetermine the range of outcomes available in the end. So, for example, opening replies from the buyer should not imply that *some* increase is acceptable; for example, an opening such as 'why?' is just as bad as 'can it be delayed?' and in both cases it implies that something could be acceptable.

Scenario 3

Your secretary has just informed you that one of your more important suppliers is on the telephone waiting to talk to you about a price increase for a range of manufactured components.

Would you:

(a) Talk to him to ascertain his position.

(b) Invite him to come and see you to discuss the matter.

(c) Tell him you are not accepting any price increases.

(d) Pretend you are not in.

(e) Ask your secretary to request that he write to you with his company's point of view.

(f) Make comparisons with the movements of other suppliers.

Answer

Option (e). The main purpose of the call is to canvass your reaction. By finding out how you react and what your position is likely to be, the other party can plan accordingly. By refusing to discuss the matter on the telephone, and instead asking the other party to write to you, you are putting the pressure on them. After you receive the letter setting out their position, you can plan how best to tackle the negotiation. It is important to avoid being conditioned by the other party, so be wary of option (b), inviting them to come in and discuss the matter: best to get their full position in writing before meeting eyeball to eyeball. Requiring a letter (or the electronic equivalent) also forces them to put down some sort of a marker, without you being committed to an immediate (or indeed any) response.

On the face of it, option (f) looks reasonable. Yet there is a danger in comparing one supplier's prices with its competitor because in practice companies often have entirely different cost structures from one another. If three suppliers offered you three different discount levels against identical starting prices you could be making a mistake by assuming that the firm offering the biggest discount level is the obvious choice. You may not be comparing apples with apples. The supplier offering the smallest discount may be a more efficient producer and you may be able to move them to offering the greatest discount: they may have more 'slack' to offer; they may overall be a more professional outfit – is the guy offering the greatest discount simply making his pricing up on the hoof?

I served as a non-executive director of a large packaging company where the main manufacturing location was in a government-sponsored economic development zone. Our cost structures were such that we could almost undercut all our competitors and still make a handsome profit, yet on many occasions the managing director's policy was not to quote the lowest price because the salespeople felt that the buyer did not intend to change suppliers whatever the case! This is an example of the buyer(s) conditioning the wrong response from the supplier.

Scenario 4

Without any warning you receive a telephone call from a large customer informing you that it is going to lengthen its payment terms from 45 to 70 days. The buyer apologizes, but says that in the current climate there is no choice.

As the credit controller would you:

(a) Ask why the buyer is having to do this.

(b) Tell the buyer that you would then be being paid much later than your average debt collection period (even if this was not true).

(c) Tell the buyer that if this is insisted on you will have to stop delivery.

(d) Propose meeting halfway at, say, 57 days.

(e) Invite the buyer to come and see you and make no comment on the phone.

(f) Visit the buyer's premises

Answer

Option (f). This reveals nothing of your position, and when the buyer is physically in front of you, some of the other options may be used. You keep the customer guessing about your reaction. The information gathered on a visual inspection of their premises could be invaluable; for example, large work in progress or high stock levels may indicate a prosperous firm that does not need to squeeze you (or, a really good one, see if you can eyeball their scrap/rework lines! You are not required to bail out an inefficient company).

Option (c) would obviously be a somewhat crude use of power: it may succeed in the short run, but when the tables turn, as they surely will, you will be in trouble.

I take the view that any efficient company would be 'hot' on credit control and as a buyer I would only want to deal with efficient companies. Their buyer ought to respect that position.

Scenario 5

You are in a negotiation with someone you have never dealt with before. After a short introductory discussion, he suggests a compromise on the price, saying 'Let's split the difference: I'll meet you halfway, a fifty-fifty split?'

If you accept this suggestion the price you will pay would be better than you had hoped for before the meeting. Do you:

(a) Accept.

(b) Decline.

(c) Tell him his offer is insulting.

(d) Make a counter offer which is a 10 per cent movement from your starting position.

(e) Stay silent.

(f) Explain that you are looking for more.

(g) Offer to give him something he wants if he reconsiders his position.

Answer

Option (e). You have never met this person before and know nothing of his style in negotiation. If an offer is met with silence it is usually taken as rejection and an improved offer might be made. Option (c) would not be advisable; the other party has made a concession and if you dismiss it, they are unlikely to make further concessions. If you have to say something thank them for their move but tell them they must move further: it is important that the other party feels 'warm' towards you. Rejection will only turn them off.

Scenario 6

You are buying a car for cash. After some discussion with the salesperson you ask what discount is available for cash. The salesperson replies 'What did you have in mind?'
Do you:

(a) Suggest a 5 per cent discount.

(b) Suggest a 10 per cent discount.

(c) Suggest a 20 per cent discount or more.

(d) Ask the salesperson again what the cash discount is.

(e) Ask for additional items to be included in the deal at no extra cost, e.g. Sat Nav, CD player, in-car entertainment …

Answer

Option (d). Avoid putting down a 'marker' too soon. This is what the seller is trying to get you to do; a valid tactic is to ignore the question and repeat your own. This forces the seller to put a marker down (see Chapter 7).

The mistake often made by the unskilled negotiator here is to respond with a tough and large discount or percentage. However, experience shows that we can at times be very surprised by the amount that people have to give and even our tough position might not be that tough after all.

A friend of mine ran an Anglo-German electronics company supplying large blue-chip companies. On one particular range on which they had a leading reputation he sold at $1, or at the other extreme $10 per item, and indeed the $1 was usually not obtained by the buyers with the highest volumes. So in this case if you were offered $10 per unit and responded asking for a 50 per cent discount you would still be asking for a price that was well within the supplier's needs, thus creating a scenario where the pressure was very much on you and not on the other party. After all, they could accept your offer at any time as it is within their price spectrum, and you might never know how much lower you could have taken them!

Scenario 7

You are negotiating to sell a million wine glasses and have offered them to the other party at 10p each. The buyer invites you in to discuss and says, 'Your price is not good enough.'

Which of the following actions would you now take:

(a) Cut your price marginally.

(b) Defend your price.

(c) Ask what other potential suppliers are offering.

(d) Ask what price the buyer has in mind.

(e) Say that your price is competitive and there is very little you can do.

Answer

Option (d). As in Scenario 6, what you are trying to do is to get the buyer to put a marker down. This is probably lower than the buyer is prepared to settle at and your negotiating skill should increase the figure closer to yours. Option (c) could be dangerous as the buyer might tell you other suppliers' prices are lower. Option (e) would be acceptable if you stopped after the word 'competitive'. To say 'there is very little you can do' is in fact to admit that you can do something and you are signalling a concession.

Scenario 8

You have been in negotiation for a long time and you are approaching an agreement. The other party is called out of the room by a telephone call, and when he comes back he abruptly announces that he will have to terminate the negotiation and can negotiate no further. He offers you a deal if you will accept the position already reached – take it or leave it. The terms are not particularly tough, but you are giving more than you had wanted to agree to. You hoped to get more. Which of these options would you choose in answer to the ultimatum?

(a) Ask for a five-minute recess with your people.

(b) Accept the deal.

(c) Pretend you didn't hear it.

(d) Ask for time to call your boss.

(e) Try to make him feel unreasonable.

(f) Decline.

Answer

Option (e). People do not like to be thought unreasonable. It makes them feel uncomfortable. The approach, 'It seems a pity to waste all the time we have so far spent' might be appropriate. Using emotion is always a powerful approach. As an alternative you could use (a): a recess could put the pressure on the other party (see Chapter 9).

It is clear that brinkmanship is being used here and is dangerous to both parties (see Chapter 7). It is something I would almost never advise the use of. If threat is to be the tactic, I would prefer to build the threat level slowly, thus always having the option to rethink or review its effectiveness as the negotiation goes along. Reducing the scale of an implied threat can be a sign of encouragement and goodwill; abandoning a stated threat entirely looks awfully like capitulation. As with other strategies, try to subdivide the threat, so that if necessary you can make a small concession but leave the implied power of the threat intact.

Scenario 9

You are the buyer of a range of packaging items. You are in negotiation and your supplier has just surprised you with a 1 per cent reduction on the price. Which of the following would you do?

(a) Tell him to increase it to 5 per cent.

(b) Ask him if he will increase it to 5 per cent if you give him a sizeable increase in business.

(c) Make a matching concession of your own.

(d) Take a sarcastic line and tell him how sensible he was to make it.

(e) Tell him it is nothing like enough.

(f) Thank him but insist he looks again to reduce the price further.

Answer

Option (f). The other party has made a concession. He has moved towards you and your job is to keep him moving. By thanking him you take psychological possession of the concession, making it very difficult for him to withdraw it. Being sarcastic or dismissive is inappropriate for it could antagonize him and will at the very least make him 'cold' towards you. While being tough in negotiation, you should always be encouraging the other party to feel 'warm' towards you.

My research shows that unskilled negotiators are all too often derisory in response to being given something that disappoints them or simply does not meet their objectives. One of the first skills that the untrained should adopt in becoming better negotiators is to thank people for any concession, no matter how small, and to *build* and not knock down. Not only is this a fault all too common in inexperienced people but it can be readily seen in the boardroom. Alan Sugar (of *The Apprentice* on television) does his sarcastic putdowns for an audience; in real life I suspect he is a lot more sophisticated in his use of praise and thanks, blame and sarcasm.

Scenario 10

You are in a negotiation and have presented your case extremely well. The other party seem impressed but an uneasy silence has developed as they look at each other to see who is going to respond. Which of the following would you do?

(a) Go over the key points/features again.

(b) Ask them a question regarding their understanding.

(c) Turn to their lead negotiator and seek comments.

(d) Smile gently and say nothing.

(e) Fiddle with your papers to buy time.

(f) Seek an adjournment.

Answer

This scenario summarizes the presentation made by a large Western multinational to a potential customer in Japan for a 3 billion aerospace contract.

To add weight to the sales pitch the company chairman was invited to join the team. Indeed, they presented their case very well but a silence followed and although they went over the key points again the Japanese remained silent.

The chairman quickly became uneasy with the silence and filled it by asking them a question regarding understanding. When again they did not respond he offered concessions and continued doing so despite efforts to stop him … 3.5 per cent discounted off a 3 billion ten-year deal. He resigned after the next group board meeting.

Option (d). You have done all that could be expected of you: it is now up to them. Any other alternative relieves pressure. The ball is in their court: let them play it! It also emphasizes the importance of managing silence, something we are not generally good at. But this option should only be used when you know you have made an excellent job of presenting your case, so well that there is a natural pressure on the other party to respond. If your presentation had merely been good, options (a), (b) or even (c) could then be appropriate.

Let me repeat a story told in Chapter 5. A good friend of mine held the post of rector in a large parish church in England. At Remembrance Sunday service each November he held the traditional two-minute silence, but because he never wore a watch the silence never lasted more than the record-breaking 58 seconds! Silences are long even when there is no pressure on.

Scenario 11

You are selling your boat and a couple have made an offer. After the technical discussion and some exploration of price it comes to a closing phase when one of them says something like this:

(a) 'This is my final offer.'

(b) 'This is my final offer. If you don't accept it I will buy another in a couple of days.'

(c) 'This is my final offer for the boat and I will discuss the contents separately.'

(d) 'This is my final offer, here is my cheque now. It is only valid for three days.'

(e) 'This is my final offer. I can give you a cheque now.'

(f) 'This is all I can offer – take it or leave it' (in a very hard tone).

Which of these is most final and promises least hope of further negotiation?

Answer

Option (a). Any other involves a qualification of the statement which is not intended, and could give rise to an emotional reaction. The additional words after 'final offer' are there to add pressure and to most people in a negotiation indeed they would do that. However, to the trained ear they are there to add robustness because final offer is not meant in the first place. It is a form of argument dilution and is similar to answering your own questions, such as 'why do you want the price increase? Is it because your labour rates have altered or material costs, etc … ?' The skilled negotiator here will say 'No' without feeling guilty or will use the additional information in such a way as to test the veracity of the final offer position taken.

Scenario 12

You are buying a new motor car for cash. You have set your mind on one particular model and have obtained prices from three garages.

Garage	A	B	C
Price	19,995	20,100	19,600

The deal on offer from each supplier is identical in terms of added extras, delivery, colour of the car, etc. The only difference is the price. Write down what you feel would be your negotiation objective for *each* of the three garages. Give a separate price target for your negotiation with each garage.

Answer

The figure you give is less important than the fact that it should be the *same* for each garage. The deal is exactly the same, so why pay more at one than another? We must guard against being conditioned to pay a higher price merely because the opening point was higher, or because the published price has psychological pointers. 19,995 is trying to say 'We've really struggled to keep this vehicle under the 20k plus that it is really worth – this is our bargain offer.' Is it? We already know dealer C can ship the same metal for less. On the other hand, has dealer B added a few hundred on to suggest that this is not a 'bog-standard' price-sensitive saloon, but more of an aspirational purchase? In which case they might be prepared to come down quite a lot.

Scenario 13

You are in a negotiation in which you and the other party are unable to reach agreement. Both sides believe firmly in their respective positions, and in many hours each has made only token movement. What would be the order of your preference of these six possible courses of action?

(a) Change negotiators.

(b) Offer a large concession.

(c) Offer a further small concession.

(d) Change the package and scope of the negotiation.

(e) Let it go to deadlock.

(f) Be open about your feelings at the lack of movement.

Answer

This example was written after reviewing the progress of some long and detailed negotiations to amalgamate two large UK retailers. The behaviour that unlocked the impasse that had gone on for some time was the openness exhibited by option (f). Therefore, options (f), (d), (a) are the correct order of preference. Openness can be very powerful, and can put the other party under pressure to do something to relieve the situation. They are made to feel responsible for the lack of movement; hence option (f) is the first choice. Option (d) is second: the existing package will apparently produce no result and it may be worth seeing if a change will break the impasse.

However, be careful that in making a change this does not appear as a concession to the other party.

Option (a) may be worth trying since the chemistry may not be right between those currently involved in the negotiation. Changing the people may produce a result; this would be beneficial in a number of major industrial relations disputes. Sometimes, entrenched and public standpoints are genuine; if, for example, Mrs Thatcher, or union leader Arthur Scargill, the protagonist in the devastating UK miners' strike of the 1980s, said they were not budging an inch, that was it. Very often, in both labour and commercial disputes, it can appear necessary for the leader in the public eye to talk tough – to bolster a share price, to keep a union together, to attract support from other parties with similar issues – but behind the posturing there may be a quite reasonable way of negotiating a settlement. How many City takeovers start with a chairman saying in effect 'over my dead body', and end a month or two later with the same chairman proclaiming a bright new horizon for the combined operation? This is not hypocrisy, necessarily: it can often be a clever use of those celebrated one-way movers, threat and emotion. And that can work very effectively, unless the person with the high-profile public stance gets involved in the detail of two-way movers: bargains and compromises.

Scenario 14

You are a buyer for a retailer, about to enter negotiation with a manufacturer of electrical appliances. You want to reduce the seller's demands and final price as much as possible. Which option below would you choose if you planned to (1) reduce the seller's opening demand, or (2) reduce the final price?

(a) Make sure that specification(s) for the item(s) is (are) such that other manufacturers can meet it (them) easily.

(b) Ask for a quotation before the meeting: 'Please quote your lowest price.'

(c) 'Drop a few names' to indicate that you are seeking or have quotes from other suppliers.

(d) Indicate that you are seeking a long-term business relationship.

(e) Ask for a quotation for more than you will require.

(f) Place emphasis on the size of your order and the importance of supplying you.

(g) Ask for a quotation for less than you will require.

Answer

Option (a) is preferred, or second, option (g). If the specification is such that many suppliers could meet it, a highly competitive situation exists: if they want the business they will have to put in a competitive bid, hence option (a). Some buyers ask for a quotation for more than they require and then try to get the same price for a lower quantity. This antagonizes sellers and produces negative feelings: it moves them away from the 'warm' position and towards the 'cold'. If you ask for less than you actually require and you negotiate hard at that figure and then state that you actually could place an order for more, the seller clearly realizes that some price adjustment will be necessary. But at the same time he is getting more business than he thought. He now has more positive feelings and is at the 'warm' end of the scale. The move must be credible, however, in moving from what you initially ask for and what you finally order. This is the building block technique (see Chapter 11).

Scenario 15

You have been working a long time on a major sale which, if it comes off, will considerably enhance your promotion prospects. You are very close to agreement with the buyer. He now hints that he wants a personal reward for completion.

Do you:

(a) Find out what he wants?

(b) Offer him the chance to visit your factory in Nice?

(c) Ignore it?

(d) Threaten to report him to his management'?

(e) Hint at a sum of money and subsequently renege?

(f) Say you would like to help but that it is not company policy?

Answer

Option (c). Remember, this is totally unethical in Western culture, and could be just as much a threat to you as it might be to him. It may be just a 'try on' and by ignoring it you demonstrate that you are not prepared to go down that track. Or it may be that you have misunderstood what he is saying and to come down hard without further information could leave you very embarrassed indeed. At least with option (c) you have a chance to see whether he repeats the suggestion and allows you to confirm your understanding. I would advise, following a repeat of the statement from him, that you clearly summarize your understanding of what he has said. I would then suggest that you withdraw, seek an adjournment and consult back in your own organization.

Fraud and corruption (and market-rigging, for that matter) result in large fines and jail terms, and not only in Western cultures. Many less developed countries are beginning to crack down on this, and the USA, in particular, rightly or wrongly takes upon itself the right to prosecute individuals and firms with connections to the USA (the connection may simply be that US citizens are able to buy the shares) regardless of where the alleged offence was committed. The theory of extraterritorial jurisdiction is somewhat moot, but the principle that there should be no place for corruption in business life is surely sound.

Of course, 'personal rewards' requested are not necessarily monetary, or implying any loss to your own firm. In this scenario, you may get promotion if the deal goes through. The favour suggested is: 'You'll now be able to get my daughter a placement with you for her gap year – straight A*s, place for PPE at Oxford, she'll be great for your firm.' Quite possibly, but the answer has still to be the same. Do, incidentally, be wary of giving the sort of hedging answer: 'Of course I have no say in this at all, but do encourage her to send an application in.' That is an entirely true and unexceptional statement, but one that it is very easy for the other party to read a 'nudge and a wink' into.

Scenario 16

You wish to sell your boat, which cost 48,000 two years ago. Based on professional advice you would be delighted to get 39,000, although you have set a fall-back minimum of 37,500. Before you get around to putting it on the market a nodding acquaintance offers you 40,000. In response do you:

(a) Accept with alacrity?

(b) Accept?

(c) Ask for 42,000?

(d) Say you only want 39,500?

(e) Ask what he will pay for the 'extras'?

(f) Stay silent?

(g) Say you've been taken aback by his offer?

Answer

Option (g). This is an opening offer. Silence would be useful with a stranger (see earlier scenario) but would probably be an unnatural or unfriendly response to someone you know, even casually. A better way is to say something very neutral – perhaps say you did not know he was looking to buy a boat. There is then a good chance if he's serious that he will come back with an improved offer. However, you need to be careful because not having said 'No' it could be that here we have an example of the key signaller in a negotiation not being what is said but rather what is not said, i.e. *you did not say 'No'* and indicated that something along those lines was possible.

Scenario 17

You are in a negotiation with a very tough negotiator who has pushed you to concede a great deal more than you should have done. Although you know the contract will still be profitable to you at the price currently on the table, you are 2 per cent beyond your brief. You think you can sell the deal to your MD at this level but the other party wants a further concession.

Do you:

(a) Concede on a variable such as packing, delivery, payment, etc.?

(b) Ask him how much more he wants and give it to him, provided you are still convinced that your MD will agree?

(c) Ask him how much more he wants and offer to 'split the difference'?

(d) Ask for a recess?

(e) Explain that you have already exceeded your brief and have 'put your head on the block'? You must therefore return to your original opening position.

(f) Call your boss?

Answer

Option (e). This is known as re-escalation of demand (see Chapter 11). Options (a), (b) and (c) offer hope of even more concessions, which is the last thing you want. By stating that you have gone further than you should and must now retreat you demonstrate to the other party that the end has been reached: they run the risk of losing much of what they have so far achieved if they go any further and perhaps should settle before you implement your intention. Second best would have been (d). Do not use (f) as it will undermine your credibility.

Scenario 18

You are staying in a hotel for three nights while visiting an important customer whose offices are located about three miles away. The first morning you take a taxi which costs €15 for the journey. You do the same on the second morning and it costs the same. On the third morning you again take a taxi, but as the driver leaves the hotel he turns left towards the town instead of going straight on as had happened on the previous two mornings.

The journey has taken under ten minutes on previous occasions, so you wait a while to see if he is taking you a better way or one that is equally quick. After five minutes or so it becomes obvious that he is taking you out of your way. You mention your destination and ask which way he is going. He quickly apologizes and says he was dreaming, but that it will now be quicker to carry on rather than go back.

When you finally arrive at your destination do you:

(a) Ask how much the fare is?

(b) Tell him you are only paying the same as on the other two days?

(c) Say nothing, but look at him?

(d) Pay what is on the meter because he made a genuine mistake?

Answer

Option (c). Again, silence will put the onus on him to make an offer. He is at fault in going the wrong way and should offer something for the inconvenience caused. This actually happened to me. When we eventually arrived at the customer's premises, the driver apologized and said 'How much did you pay yesterday'? I remained silent. He then said 'Was it €10 or €11?' The pressure was on him to make a very reasonable offer, having wasted my time. Of course the amounts were small but the principle is important: silence can be a potent weapon in negotiation.

Scenario 19

Your house is on the market. After a quiet period with no potential buyers, a couple finally agrees to view the property. After inspecting the whole house they look at you and say, 'It's not quite what we wanted and we would have to spend a lot of money on redecoration, but we might be able to come to a deal if you accept a reduction of 20,000.' What are your choices?

Answer

The buyers have taken a tone showing that long-term relationships are not important (unsurprisingly as this is obviously a one-off negotiation. That would be the case in most house sales, although not all: if you are keeping the big house and selling off the granny annexe, relationships with potential buyers probably do need to be looked at longer term). All in though, the fact that they have made you an offer shows interest and represents good news. You must not be put off by the prickly tone and focus on the phrase 'not quite what we wanted' … but the signal is possibly that it is largely what they do want!

The buyers are trying to make you feel uncomfortable and have put in a bid below the asking price. Although you have had your house on the market for some time you should not be too eager here, for it could be that they are more desperate than you.

Some questioning would not go amiss!
But do not say 'No' unless you want to send them in a negative direction. You need to check out the buyers' situation and try and make them feel warm. You could begin with 'Are you able to move quickly?' or 'Are you in a chain?' This will help you to gather information about their personal circumstances.

You could counter their comments about the decoration with use of emotion. 'It's a shame you don't like the decoration. It was something we took a lot of care about. Well, everyone has their own taste. How would you change it?' Now you can get them to start talking about 'how' they would change it rather than 'if' they buy the house. Try to replace 'if' with 'when'.

You know the price range in your area. What is your first offer? You might offer a discount if they can offer you something: a fast move, payment for the carpet or curtains, etc. You should have your variables ready and try to trade them, but first go for one-way movement.

Using something they may construe as threatening, such as: 'You are the third couple this morning', conditions them to think that the house is popular and that you will not accept a much reduced offer. You also have the fall-back of blaming the balance due to the bank or building society for your not being able to accept their offer.

'We might be able to entertain a small discount' could start the ball rolling. Be prepared for their answer because they may well say, 'How much can you accept, then?' You are going to have to put down a marker at this stage.

Remember to start low (in terms of discount of course, not of price). One or two thousand is a good starting point (but not both figures) and will not damage your credibility. You want to condition them to be thinking in thousands and not tens of thousands for the discount.

You may decide to move slowly towards them and make the deal. You may have to walk away. Whatever you do, do not be put off with a 'take it or leave it' approach (the answer is to leave it) and remember that the deal does not have to be done on the spot. They can always come back, provided you work to leave them feeling warm and neither party takes anything personally.

House sales and purchases are, for most of us, the most financially significant personal negotiations we will ever experience. Houses are also very personal: for the seller there are memories, for the buyer, dreams. The scenario above assumes reasonably stable prices, which in recent history has not always been the case: prices have soared and, at the time of writing, have slumped. Either way, there is pressure on one party or the other to 'grab what they can'. Newspapers and television channels are full of advice, some helpful, much of it self-serving (of communities such as estate agents). Ask yourself, whether you are buying or selling, 'If this deal was as relatively important to my company's well-being or survival as it is to my family's, how would I approach it, and how is that different from the way I am negotiating here?' If there is some major mismatch, you really need to have a serious think about what you are doing.

Scenario 20

You do your preparation for the negotiation and the process begins. After a short period the other side makes an offer far in excess of your 'wow!' What is your response?

Answer

If your preparation was done properly you may have been truly fortunate here. What you might ask at this stage is whether your preparation was not a little skimpy and your 'wow!' was not set high enough.

I remember taking my daughter Emma with me to buy a family touring caravan. The sales person predictably asked me what price I wanted for my old caravan in part exchange. I was ready not to put a marker down (see Chapter 7) and asked the salesperson what they were prepared to offer. The figure he stated was way above what I expected after considerable research. I had discussed what I had expected with my teenage daughter beforehand and now, before I could stop her, she turned to me and said: 'Dad, that's a lot more than you thought isn't it?' Oops!

It may be, though, that your homework was correct and the other party has made a palpable error. In this case you should refrain from doing a lasting deal until you have checked the figures very carefully. It may also be that the other side is experiencing business problems which have caused them to put together a desperate (and maybe untenable) deal.

None the less, you have been pleasantly surprised and need to react. What you must *not* do here is to accept the offer. It is a well-known tenet of negotiating that you never accept the first offer, so you can reasonably assume that the other party still has plenty left to offer.

Using the 'thank and bank' principle you should obtain ownership of the offer by thanking them for it. At the same time you should try to warm up the other party by talking to them about other issues related to the sale and illustrating that good progress is being made. You must also make it very clear that they still have some way to go before the offer can be finally accepted.

You may have to offer them something in return for further movement if you feel that the opportunities for one-way movement have been exhausted, but your planning should have taken care of that.

The key points of this dilemma are to aim high, be cautious and be flexible in achieving as much as you can get, rather than aiming at any particular number. However, be careful if you are in a team with colleagues that none of them undermines your position like my teenage daughter did!

Scenario 21

You are looking for a price reduction but the other party produces a large amount of statistical evidence concerning rising raw material prices and wage inflation. How do you counter these arguments?

Answer

This is a comparatively simple situation. You are into the use of logic and the tactics are straightforward.

If you know that 'proof'' is likely to be a key issue make sure that you get yours in first. You have already lost the initiative here because you have allowed the other party to tell you 'why' before you have had the chance to tell them 'why not'.

It is a simple but effective rule that the person who fires first in a logic war has the advantage. Get your logic in first and let them 'pick' over your case.

Your reply to comments concerning raw materials, prices and inflation should be along the lines of, 'I appreciate all your arguments, but if I can't accept it, that's all there is to say.'

Let them justify their prices. You merely have to reply that you will not stretch to the new amount. You could then try a hint of threat with something like, 'I know you think you can justify your new prices but it would be a shame if it was this price rise that drove us to consider a fundamental new approach to your product.'

It may be possible to try to beat some of their logic with some of your own, but you must be well prepared and ready to fight them on their own ground. They will have done all their homework and it will show if you have not. An adjournment may be necessary.

You could try some argument dilution. Listen to their arguments and get them to put down as many of their reasons as possible. Your hope is that finally they will present one that is weak enough for you to attack. Logical reasoning can be a 'one-way mover' and you need to avoid any signals from your position that hint at partial or total acceptance … nodding as you go along with their apparently sound ideas.

Scenario 22

You are faced with a very low reactor who says absolutely nothing and seems to enjoy long silences and showing nothing in body language either. How do you react?

Answer

Low reactors are difficult negotiators to meet across the table. The ability to sit and say nothing is truly a powerful behaviour. Think of spy movies: the part in John le Carre's *Tinker Tailor Soldier Spy*, where the young George Smiley (played by Alec Guiness) faces Soviet spy Karla across the table in a Delhi prison. It's a long scene – Smiley tries everything from the book – indeed from this book: emotion, threat, logic, bargaining. Karla says nothing, in voice or body. Smiley not only loses that encounter, but is permanently affected. (OK, two books later he achieves a sort of victory, but in commercial life we cannot wait that long!) In other scenes, Smiley himself is quite an exponent of the long silence which his opponent feels must be filled.

In most situations in a negotiation the more you say the more you give away. That is why questioning is such a useful technique. This, then, is the arena of the low reactor.

When silence is starting to become almost insufferable the low reactor seems to be able to sit there without feeling any discomfort or embarrassment. In any battle of nerves these people can sit poker-faced.

Once you have identified these attributes you can then begin to copy them. If you know that you are by nature a gregarious character you must curb your natural instincts to be talkative.

Experienced negotiators have a great deal of self-knowledge. They are aware of those traits that come naturally to them and those that require effort. You must seek to do the same. Know your strengths and weaknesses and when you come up against particular characters identify the situation and react accordingly.

Low reactors say little and enjoy silence. Be like them even if it feels uncomfortable. That will be your successful first move in the exchange.

Be very careful of giving concessions. Consider a recess to help you … and another and another.

Scenario 23

After a spell of exchanging information it seems you are going to have to put down your marker first. How might you do this with minimum damage?

Answer

First of all, are you sure that you really have to put down the first marker? Try to avoid it, but if it would damage your credibility to withhold the bid you will have to make the first move.

One way to minimize the damage is to place your marker hypothetically. You might use an expression like: 'OK, if you want a price I'll give you one, but I don't think that you'll be impressed.' Similar is: 'I can give you a number, but I know from what you've said that it's probably more than you wanted to pay.'

Comments like these allow you to put down a very high marker without damaging your credibility. If you call it a 'high bid' yourself you can agree with the other party then offer, 'Well what did you have in mind?' This gives you an opportunity to get a number from them.

Consider variables such as discounts or rebates, rather than just price. What would a trained car salesperson offer? A free service, insurance, metallic paint, etc. … anything other than putting down a marker! Also refer to Chapter 7, page 51 and Chapter 10, page 117.

Scenario 24

The other party in the negotiation tells you that just one small move from you will clinch the deal. Do you believe them and how do you react?

Answer

This dilemma hinges on two points. The first is the definition of the word 'small' and the second is whether you believe them.

'One small step' has become an often used phrase. You will need to ask what exactly they have in mind. Remember to ask here, as it is vital to get them to define what they mean by 'small' before you put in your version. Size is often only a matter of opinion: how big is an economy size car? How big is an economy size box of breakfast cereal?

Once they have told you what it is you have to do to clinch the deal you can then progress. You may be pleasantly surprised and more than able to meet their demands.

Of course, the next point then becomes important. It may be that even when you have given them what they want they then try the Colombo tactic (named after the famous TV detective). This is when someone asks you for 'just one more small thing' right at the end of the negotiation when you thought everything was agreed ... and keeps asking and asking.

Be careful. Verify that if you meet the demand you really will have a deal. This will make it clear to the other party that they will damage their credibility if they do not then move straight into an agreement.

Scenario 25

You are constantly being interrupted by an argumentative adversary. This is causing you concern and the negotiation is beginning to stall. What do you do?

Answer

First we need to make some tactical decisions.

■ Is the negotiation going your way?

■ Is this person actually shooting themselves in the foot?

■ Are you happy with the negotiation continuing in this fashion even though you find it unusual?

If the answer to any of these questions is 'No' then you need to do something about it. There is a range of options. If you need to break into the conversation then try to drive in a wedge to allow this to happen. The best way is with a behaviour label: signal your intention to do something before actually beginning. In this example it would be something like, 'I wonder if I could just break in for a moment – I'd like to ask a question?'

This sentence should be accompanied by a firm gesture, a smile and strong eye contact. This leaves the other party in no doubt about your serious intention. If they then ignore you, you must have the assertiveness to continue and make it clear that you do not intend to back down on this point.

Have your questions arranged in advance. It will allow you to fire them off at key moments so that you gain control of the conversation. Most people feel the need to answer a question when one is asked, which allows you to drive the conversation in the direction that you desire.

You could also use emotion and let the other party know that you feel the negotiation is not making the progress it should and that you both need to rethink the agenda or perhaps take a recess.

It is a recurring theme that if you reward bad behaviour by the other party then all that you will receive in return is more bad behaviour. You must let the other party know that there is a downside to their poor behaviour. As always this must be said in an appropriately professional tone. If that sounds a little like training a puppy, that is no coincidence: people are also animals, and react as such.

Scenario 26

You are in a difficult position and the tide is flowing against you. What options are open to you?

Answer

Much here depends on experience and confidence. If you have the ability to carry it off then you might try to be open and just a little theatrical and say something like, 'Look, I'm feeling hurt and attacked here. This is going to cost me and I'm not going to be able to continue if you keep trying to back me into a corner.'

If you do it correctly you may be able to get the other party to reply with 'Why, what's wrong?' which suddenly now puts you back in the action with a long piece of well-considered logic.

Another option is to go for an adjournment. It may be better to bring the meeting to a premature conclusion in order to regroup and rethink than to continue when things are going so badly. It may be that a shorter recess could help initially.

Why not try to put this issue on the backburner, so that you can get to an agenda that suits you? Obviously you cannot require the other party to acquiesce to this, but it might be worth trying. This shows the value of planning both your arguments before the negotiation and the running order of the agenda. Be aware, though, that what you can do to the other party, they can do to you (see also Scenario 17).

Scenario 27

You have just managed to extract movement from the other party on a 'final' position. What do you do as a result of this?

Answer

Good negotiators never show triumph and you should not now, even though you have secured a substantial advantage in the negotiation.

You now know that the other party will move from a 'final' offer. This means that if they will move from one 'final' offer then they are more than likely to move from the next one and the next one after that.

This is one of the small pieces of knowledge gleaned during a negotiation that allows you to build up a picture of both the nature of the deal and, more importantly, the other person.

Your next move will be to test the other party. Now that you know that they may be able to move further than you perhaps suspected you can probe areas of opportunity. These will centre on the major variables of the negotiation.

You have been conditioned by this one poor piece of behaviour to assume that much more movement may be possible than first thought. This reveals how vulnerable you become if you allow the other party to believe that you have more to give away.

How often have we seen high-profile negotiations where one party or the other, via the media, states a final position only to move again, often as a result of threat or the use of power?

Thinking in real time is important. Never say anything unconsidered that may come back to haunt you.

Scenario 28

The negotiator opposite insists that he has exceeded his limits and will need to call his boss for further advice. How do you react?

Answer

This could be both good news and bad. The good news is that you now know that the real decision maker is back at the office. You know the person you are dealing with does not have total authority, a fact you should have discussed sooner.

You should try to discover the identity of the decision maker and perhaps deal direct. This could be advantageous if you feel that the person with whom you are negotiating is really too junior for you to be able to reach a proper conclusion. This may, however, lead to antagonism between the other party and yourself if he feels he is being undermined. You could destroy the relationship if they feel undervalued.

The bad news might be that this is merely a ploy to buy some space in the negotiation. He might need some time for thinking or extra planning.

It might be that the other side intends to use the 'boss' character as a lever against you. 'My boss won't let me go any higher' allows the other negotiator to remain your 'friend' and directs your unhappiness towards the boss. It is amazing in these situations how often the boss is unavailable for meetings with you. Should this occur you can use both emotion and logic to undo the tactic. Feelings of being let down by the other party or perhaps a need to send more information to the boss by fax or email can start to unpick it – and very quickly, nowadays. 'Look, I've got my BlackBerry – let's get your boss's thoughts right now' is a good bluff-caller. Ultimately, 'the boss' is often a ploy and you should treat it as such.

The best way, of course, is to ascertain the extent of the other party's authority at the start of the negotiation and insist on going to see the source of authority if you can. If it transpires that your opposite number has been claiming authority that he or she does not really possess, that may open up other opportunities.

Scenario 29

Your counterpart across the table suddenly loses their temper and becomes most unpleasant. What options do you have and how can you exploit the situation to your advantage?

Answer

When this happens in a negotiation the one thing to keep in mind is the absolute need not to get angry, unless planned (a staged display of anger, as opposed to actually being angry, can be effective. Older readers may remember Nikita Kruschev of the USSR banging his shoe on the table at the United Nations. No way was that a spontaneous gesture, but it got his message around the world). You should not allow the other party to put you off by their bad behaviour. *They are the victim at this point.*

With your control maintained you act firmly and assertively. In a quiet manner you can look the other party in the eye, smile in a friendly way and make it very clear that their behaviour is not going to cause you to move on any major negotiation variables.

Choose words such as 'I can see that you are very passionate about this issue, but I must say that it doesn't shake me from my commitment that …'

You might be a little firmer with something like 'I'm sorry to have to say that I'm finding this negotiation to be a bit heated for my taste. Why don't we take a break for ten minutes …?' You then get up and make it clear that you are taking the break, even if the other party does not agree.

At each stage make it clear that you are not going to be a soft touch and that bullying tactics will not work. If you are presented with inappropriate language then you have every right to make it plain (in a firm and friendly manner) that you would prefer if such language was not used.

Make your point without raising the temperature of the negotiation.

Scenario 30

Author's note: This case study is more detailed than those that have gone before. I have included it because it involves four different parties and made the main headlines in many international newspapers. I have included an extract from a professional journal to develop the background for the reader.

Introduction

With friends like these ... who needs competitors?

You are a senior purchasing executive for a major international airline and you have been left with egg on your face after a well-publicized (newspapers and television) problem with your airline's catering partner. There are serious questions over your sourcing strategy and the supplier's fundamental ability to meet it with their current business objectives, i.e. a clear mismatch and no overlap in the negotiating spectrum.

It is tempting to look on the problem as just one of those things. After all, it is not every day that staff dismissals made by an outsourcing partner spark unofficial strike action resulting in a customer service meltdown and a raft of embarrassing publicity.

To quote from a leading professional journal:

Was it just an isolated case, a risk that fell outside parameters of what could reasonably be anticipated and managed?

On reflection, the answer has to be a resounding no. Various pieces of research – from the UK, Europe, the US and Australia – have focused on the thorny question of whether outsourcing works. The conclusion has been that it usually does not, with various estimates putting the failure rate at between 40 and 80 per cent. Far too often the benefits described in the initial business case for an outsourcing arrangement never actually get delivered.

Given this disappointing backdrop, perhaps it is time to get back to some fundamentals. A number of immutable principles underpinning successful outsourcing have emerged over the past 20 years:

- ■ Be clear what you want to do and why you want to do it.

- Undertake a comprehensive risk assessment.

- Ensure you have a deep understanding of supply markets and suppliers.

- Understand what suppliers are trying to achieve with your business – and what really motivates them.

- Work hard to build and then manage effective business relationships.

- Negotiate a watertight contract.

- Plan and ensure effective project management of the transition phase from internal to external operation.

Examining the problem the airline faced in the light of these basic 'success or fail' indicators provides a number of interesting insights. Firstly, what was it trying to achieve? Evidence suggests that at least part of the drive to outsource was based on achieving significant cost reductions. But cases from around the world show just how hard it can be for organizations to tackle their true internal costs and deliver genuine savings through outsourcing. And without a clear handle on internal costs, and with a service that is so customer-sensitive and central to the brand, is it even appropriate to build a case for outsourcing based solely on this tricky and ambiguous ground?

It may be that it sensed an opportunity to resolve some of its longstanding industrial relations difficulties. If so, it's unclear how this issue was expected to resolve itself on the ground, with broadly the same people working in the same location in close proximity to friends and relatives who remained employees of the airline. Take the supplier's very different management culture and throw into the mix its takeover by a venture capital firm, and you hardly have the ideal recipe for industrial relations harmony.

Perhaps the main drive to outsource was in support of some grand corporate strategy that saw the company as somehow divided into 'core' as opposed to 'non-core' business processes. Perhaps management corridors at the time echoed to: 'We're an airline not a catering company!' Blind business dogma.

An all-too-common factor in the most painful outsourcing cases is the complete absence of supply chain risk assessment – both upfront and on an ongoing basis. In this case, one potentially productive area for risk assessment might have been to assess the implications of the purchase of the supplier by venture capitalists and their inevitable objectives for the business. Clearly some risks are likely to occur when a buyer's price-driven procurement approach clashes with a supplier backed by investors who are demanding a 30 per cent return on their investment.

To compound matters, it is by no means clear whether a coherent approach was implemented to what is currently known as strategic relationship management (SRM). Delivering a good quality food and drink service is clearly something of high strategic importance to an airline – it is something that is integral to the customer's experience and can therefore have a significant impact on how its brand is perceived. Yet this does not appear to have been reflected in the relationship and performance management style adopted. Indeed, the default relationship approach to the caterer seems to have been a combination of aggressive 'price down' negotiations coupled with what was recently described by a senior airline executive as 'tough love'!

None of this should be seen as some kind of perfect-world mantra demanding the unachievable. Though they appear to be in the minority, effective procurement teams around the world deploy these sort of best-practice approaches every day. Only by joining them can organizations succeed at outsourcing, enhancing their brands and creating value in the process. Otherwise they will drift towards the stricken majority for whom outsourcing becomes a path to accelerating value destruction and brand damage.

So you have catering staff on strike, a catering partner who clearly is being asked by the parent company for more profit and no food on your aeroplanes!

What went wrong and what options do you have for this negotiation?

Answer

The challenge here is to identify the behavioural approach taken by the airline, which at other times might have been appropriate with different ownership of the supplier, and decide the approach which should have been taken and the variables or innovations necessary to avoid serious brand value damage.

To complicate matters there are potentially four organizations involved in this negotiation, i.e. the airline, the supplier, the venture capitalist who owns the supplier and the trade union.

The mismatch is usefully considered by referring to the models in Appendix 1. Also refer to Chapter 8 to consider the type of relationship. Ask yourself what the caterer wanted from the airline and vice versa. Also look at negotiating styles and rules for use.

Conclusion: Practical Cases

The last scenario makes an excellent real-life problem on which to conclude this short case studies chapter. The answers are for the reader to debate and develop from all the advice given in the previous chapters and above all else show the absolute necessity for variations in approach as markets change and supplier status moves. I have seen so often supply partnerships fail because of inappropriate negotiating behaviour and indeed Mari Sako (at the London School of Economics) wrote about this approach to business and reasons for failure in such key supply relationships. Debate the case studies with colleagues and use them for practical training sessions.

14

Checklists for Success ... For When You Are Short of Time

The purpose of this chapter is to act as a ready reference for the negotiator in a hurry. It serves as a reminder of some key dos and don'ts which may make the difference between success or failure in your next negotiation. The last section is a short contingency plan for someone who is *really* in a hurry and has only, say, five minutes in which to prepare. If the negotiation is important and you do not even have this much time then it would be unwise to proceed. Negotiate instead for a postponement and recognize that if the other party resists then this may only be their tactic for applying pressure.

Negotiation – Some Dos

Be clear about your point of view. Negotiation is about moving the other party to come round to your way of thinking, to win them over to your point of view. You cannot be effective if you do not have a clear picture of your own position. It often helps to say out loud to yourself what you believe to be your 'rights' in the situation ... but remember that the world does not owe you a living, so you must persuade it to see things your way.

Dig in early on, on a big issue, and stick close to your position. The effort of doing so begins to alter the other party's expectation of the final deal which is to be struck.

Work out the relative bargaining power of yourself and of the other party. If you have power, use it carefully and gently at first. Take care that if you use power to get your own way, then sooner or later they will do the same with you, perhaps on the next deal. You will have taught them how to deal with you.

Try to get into a position where you do not have to use the bargaining mode of negotiation. Never betray by the merest gesture that you are willing to trade. Take a posture and stick to it as long as possible. Remember that only two of the approaches we have outlined involve you giving up part of your position: bargaining and compromise. The other methods – logic, coercion, emotion – all have the potential to win the other party completely over to your position without you moving.

Trade or bargain on the 'straw' issues. If you have to trade do so only on the minor issues. Make these issues appear important, for example by only trading them and never giving them away. Go through the motions of bargaining and allow the other party to 'win' concessions.

The scout's motto: 'Be prepared'. Preparation and planning are important. We never have enough time. However, there is generally no difference in the time allocated to this phase of negotiation by average and successful negotiators. The difference is in the type of planning. Successful negotiators balance their time between process (how) and task (what) issues, rather than concentrating on task issues only.

Manage your team. If you are not alone then allocate tasks:

- calculations

- tracking concessions

- opportunities.

Avoid at all costs the person who has not been *listening* and jumps in with both feet to undermine your case.

Make the other party compete. Try to avoid premature commitment to their product or service. Keep them selling because their propensity to make concessions will be greater. Hiding the true quantity you want to buy is another way of making them compete. Selectivity and variation in timing of purchase will also help.

Recess. Use this tactic to avoid the early close or premature pressure to commit, to consider/review difficult issues and to make even the shortest of calculations, especially when a calculator is involved. Never feel bad about it. Time the recess to maximum effect.

Integrity rather than complete openness. A good negotiator does not reveal his total hand, nor does he tell the complete story of what he wants or why he wants it. A good negotiator reveals information in small pieces, as and when it is necessary. He hides from his opponents feelings about the objectives he has been set to achieve; having said that, he must provide an anchor for the other party. If he makes a commitment it has to hold. If the other party distrusts the negotiator he will be nervous or anxious and may withdraw. He will almost certainly become more difficult to deal with. A good negotiator must be *trustworthy*.

Listen, rather than talk. We are all inclined to waffle and wave the flag; we keep talking to show what good negotiators we are and to display our knowledge. If we lack confidence it helps to keep up

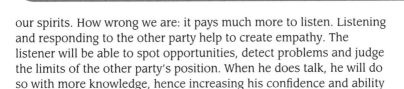

our spirits. How wrong we are: it pays much more to listen. Listening and responding to the other party help to create empathy. The listener will be able to spot opportunities, detect problems and judge the limits of the other party's position. When he does talk, he will do so with more knowledge, hence increasing his confidence and ability to ask good questions.

Summarize. Do so regularly and not just at the end. Sum up the points you like and weaken the other party's position by ignoring or playing down those you do not like. Use it to illustrate the concessions you need: 'If you can do this and this, then we ...'

Lend a helping hand. If the other party gets himself into a deep hole it can pay well, on occasions, to give him a ladder. A small investment for a larger return.

Aim high. The more you ask for the more you get. It pays to make high demands. However, a posture must be credible. Too high, and you will achieve deadlock or the other party may withdraw. Very high demands need to be tentatively signalled to the other party in order to test reaction and set up expectations. The higher you aim the more likely the other party is to ask you 'Why?' So have a response prepared, but it does not necessarily have to be a case based on logic. Emotions and feelings can just as effectively support an ambitious target. 'I feel your prices are far too high' and 'When you stopped deliveries in order to force us to pay your price increase you badly damaged the relationship between our companies' are powerful expressions of feeling if stated assertively. What price confidence? What price hurt pride?

Use the building block technique. Each negotiable issue is a card in your hand: do not play them all at once. Play the cards singly and get a concession from the other party each time, e.g. get the best price for a smaller volume, then a reduction for larger volume over the year, then two years, and so on. Too many buyers offer 'good news' to the supplier even before the negotiation has begun: 'Before we start let me say that we are now looking for twice the volume and a three-year contract!'

Elicit offers ... do not make them. Get the other party to reveal their targets, or what 'they think is reasonable'. Use 'What if ...' or 'Just supposing ...' questions if they do not respond to a direct approach. Reveal your expectations too soon and you will never know what they *might* have offered, which might have been better.

Say thank you! Always thank the other party for any concessions they offer. This is part of being 'warm' and courteous but, more importantly, establishes that you have received and taken ownership of what was offered. If this is not done there is the real danger that the concession will be taken back. Saying thank you does not stop you from asking for more, but it means that you can place your foot firmly on the next stepping stone towards your goal.

Authority. Ensure that you understand the levels and extent of your authority in the areas in which you are to negotiate. The tactics of 'removed authority' or 'defence in depth', that is removing or strictly limiting authority, can be beneficial if not declared to the other party.

Negotiation – Some Don'ts

Don't make things easy for the other party. People derive more satisfaction from things they have worked hard to get. Give the other party this satisfaction. However, at the end make it a little better than they thought it was going to be.

Don't compromise early in the meeting. Compromise will favour the party who postures more extremely. Use it only to break an impasse or bridge a 'last gap'.

Don't always leave the important issues to the middle or end of the agenda. To do so is the predictable behaviour of the average negotiator, often resulting in lack of time on the important issues.

Never, ever show triumph. The sting in the tail. We have all seen the negotiator who lost and said little, but seethed with anger and determined to beat the other party, if not destroy him, the next time.

Don't feel too successful. Bernard Shaw once said, 'Success is the brand on the brow of the person who aimed too low.' Are we successful? Was our need to feel successful strong? Was our perception of what was possible lowered?

Don't paint yourself or the other party into a corner. Leave yourself room. Good negotiators do not use 'either or', they use 'if and then'. A cornered animal can be dangerous. Never ask 'What is your lowest price?' 'Is that the best you can do?'

Don't go it alone on protracted or complex negotiations. To negotiate and remain objective is very difficult. To have a partner who remains objective can be beneficial. Besides the obvious advantage of increased security, another person can, for example:

- decide when a recess is relevant

- plot concessions made by the parties

- listen for signals – sometimes what is not said rather than what is said.

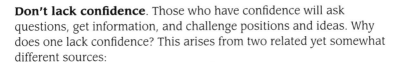

Don't lack confidence. Those who have confidence will ask questions, get information, and challenge positions and ideas. Why does one lack confidence? This arises from two related yet somewhat different sources:

- the fear of losing and looking foolish
- the fear of facing an experienced opponent.

Both can be avoided by knowledge: preparing your groundwork thoroughly and the knowledge that you are a trained, skilled negotiator. Lack of confidence often results from fear that a mistake might be made. It is a pity because we learn more from our mistakes. Remember that the making of a mistake is not a final defeat: it can be rectified without damage to one's negotiating position.

Don't get sidetracked. The use of side-issues is a classical tactical ploy. Do not wander, unless you intend to do so. Your opponent will try to sidetrack you if he considers he is losing a particular point under discussion or that a telling point is about to be made against him. Be on your guard! The 'backburner' is a useful counter-tactic.

Don't 'bridge'. Saying phrases like '3 or 4 per cent' or '4 or 5 years' not only signals uncertainty on your part but also allows the other party to choose the number that suits them best and then concentrate on it.

Don't be greedy. A negotiator needs to push hard then grab that result or opportunity and not try for something his opponent will never give. By being greedy you risk losing all. Do not take that risk.

Don't move quickly. A slow concession pattern is a trait of a good negotiator. Go for the most you can get and do not come off this top limit of your aspirations too easily. To do anything else signals an initial demand that was too strong and motivates your opponent to push you down.

An Emergency Plan for those Preparing in a Rush

1 Remember that *everything* is negotiable, even time. Postpone the negotiation if you need more time.

2 Your job is to get the other party to see things *your* way.

3 Be clear in your own mind about what *is* your point of view. If necessary say it out loud to yourself.

4 Think of a case that fits each of the five methods of negotiation.

5 Be warm and tough: be friendly and courteous, and remember there is a place for humour and for thanks.

6 Set high but defensible targets and communicate them in personal terms.

15

Cue Cards – Aides-Mémoire

You have now worked through 14 chapters. You may have been a very good negotiator before starting this book, in which case I hope you will have picked up some ideas to help you to be even more effective. You will have been able to check out your style and review appropriate rules and tactics.

If you started out as something less than an expert you will have learnt something about what an expert does and how they think and feel. This should help you in the long run and give you confidence.

Aeroplane pilots use checklists during take-off and landing and they follow them rigorously so that they do not miss the obvious. Likewise skilled negotiators use checklists to ensure that they do not miss something important. Very often when I have been called in to assist where a negotiation has gone wrong for an organization I find that the problem came about because they missed an important step.

The cue cards that follow are your checklist for future negotiations. Copy them, adapt them, but above all use them.

Now negotiate, practise, and confidence will grow; don't and your ability will diminish. Try to negotiate outside the commercial context: at a car boot sale, a street market at home or overseas, with a hotel against their normal charges or with somebody who has given you less than satisfactory service. If you do you will realize that what I have advocated in this book actually works.

Computers will never negotiate for you; they will never get someone to do something they do not want to using non-violent means. People will still tell lies in the years ahead and in business opportunistic behaviour will abound so people and organizations will need to negotiate more than ever.

Preliminary Preparation and Planning

- Avoid going into a commercial negotiation underplanned and underprepared.

- It is better to postpone the meeting and delay the business rather than try to negotiate by instinct.

- You should ask yourself if you need to negotiate at all. Is there another process available? Would sealed bids be more effective?

Ask yourself the following questions:

- Is this a real negotiation?

- Is the other side willing to negotiate?

- Am I prepared to do a deal if the terms are right?

- What are my authority levels?

- How long do I wish this process to last?

- Do I know what will happen next after this negotiation and have I planned for it?

- Am I the only person involved?

If in a team negotiation you need to make sure that every person involved is properly briefed and informed.
Team members need to **listen**.

- Who will you be negotiating against?

- Do you know the people individually?

- Have you formulated any ideas about how you might treat each individual?

- If you don't have this information how will you obtain it?

- Where is the venue for the negotiation?

- Is it at their place or yours?

- Would a neutral venue be better?

- Have you seen the room in advance?

- What about the seating plan?

- Are you aware of breaks in the meeting for refreshments or meals?

Objective Setting

- Have a **clear** idea of what you expect to achieve from the negotiation.

- This does not mean 'fixed targets' but rather a planned range within which the negotiation should fall.

- Look closely at all of the numbers in the deal and place against each set of numbers a three-stage range.

- This will ensure that you do not sit back and relax too quickly when a simple, not very stretching target has been achieved in the early stages of the negotiation.

The Three-Stage Range

1. Ideal

- What would you like to achieve if you were to have the most favourable set of circumstances?

- It is unlikely that you would achieve this but you must not suffer from a lack of ambition.

- Understand that an ideal that is placed foolishly high could damage your credibility, so it is important not to reveal it.

2. Realistic

- You seriously desire to achieve this.

- Be sensible and you can justify this both to yourself and to the other party if necessary.

- This represents what you would be only moderately satisfied to achieve.

- Your ambitions are higher than this but you may have to go this low if circumstances go against you.

3. Fall-back

- This is your lowest set of numbers. If you cannot achieve better than this then you will not be able to deal.

- It is important in any negotiation to have a position planned beyond which you cannot do business.

- It may be that you are locked into a situation whereby you cannot realistically walk away. In that case you must stress to the other party the long-term negative consequences of forcing you to deal when you are reluctant.

These three outcomes should exist as options in all negotiations.

Know the Other People

■ What do you know about the other people in the deal?

■ How many people will be involved?

■ Will this be a team negotiation or will you be in against a single opponent?

■ What are the personal and business interests of the individual people with whom you will be dealing?

■ Do they have any particular areas of activity for which they are well known and about which you should have knowledge?

■ What are the likely courtesies to be?

■ Is it likely to be friendly and have you considered which tone you should take in order to strike the right note?

■ What are the cultural, geographical or social backgrounds of the other side?

■ Will you have to make any adjustments because of this?

■ Who is the boss or decision maker on the other side?

■ Do you know their management structure?

■ Are you sure that you are talking to the right person? You could be wasting your time if you are not talking at the right level.

■ Are there any problems from previous meetings that may need to be overcome?

■ Are you sure that you have no skeletons that may haunt you in the first few minutes of the meeting?

■ What limits do the other party have on them?

■ Can they agree on the spot or will they have to refer?

■ Are you prepared for an adjournment and do you have dates ready for a follow-up meeting?

Organize your Variables

■ The variables in a negotiation are those items that can be traded, conceded or bargained away as the give and take of the deal unfolds.

■ It is important to ensure that you do not enter a negotiation without having identified all of your variables, put a value on them and created a three-stage range on the price of each one.

■ You must also draw up a list of the variables that the other side will want to trade. You should try to prioritize both your variables and theirs to see which are the most important.

■ You must try to see what value the other side will place on these same variables. Obviously you wish to trade something that is 'cheap' for you in return for something that has value. You may find that you have something that cost you nothing which the other side will pay highly for.

Some ideas for negotiation variables:

Advertising	Exclusivity	Payment terms	Servicing
Audit rights	Free samples	Performance guarantee	Sole supplier
Buy-back agreement	Guarding and security	Price	Spares
Cash payment	Guinea-pig customer	Price stability	Specification
Currency	Health and safety	Price variation formula	Supply security
Confidentiality	Indemnity	Pro forma invoice	Terms and conditions
Consignment stock	Installation	Product endorsement	Test runs
Consultancy	Insurance	Promotions	Third party liability
Contract length	International contracts	Quality	Tool kits
Customization	Installation costs	Quantity	Training
Deferral of price rises	Lead time	Referrals	Translations

Advertising	Exclusivity	Payment terms	Servicing
Delivery costs	Liquidated damages	Relationship	Trail batch
Delivery frequency	Maintenance	Reliability	Visits to competitors
Delivery locations	Manuals	Retrospective discounts	Visits to customers
Discounts	Most favoured nation	Returnable packaging	Volume
Emergency response	Packaging	Risk sharing	

Map the Route

Avoid entering into a negotiation without having drawn up a very careful route map of the direction and destination of the meeting and any subsequent events.

A negotiation has very clear phases and these must be planned.

The route may not be completely sequential; you may have to backtrack but at least you will be prepared.

Negotiation can be viewed in four main phases:

- **Opening**

- **Testing**

- **Moving**

- **Agreeing.**

- The opening phase is when you first enter the room.

- Each party needs to greet the other and it is at this stage first impressions are made.

- Be careful not to expose your business objectives too quickly.

- The testing phase is when you need to check that all of your planning and preparation has not been founded on faulty assumptions. Question to 'test'.

- The moving phase is when you need to extract concessions from the other party and perhaps trade variables.

- The final phase is the setting of the deal.

■ Quite often this will involve some symbolic shaking of hands and/
or the exchange of a written agreement.

The Opening Phase

Creating Rapport

Make a good first impression. You must ensure that you manage
your behaviour through this initial period so that you can capitalize
later on the goodwill that this will create.

Here is a list of simple behaviours that will ensure that you
always manage to do the very best for yourself when you first meet
somebody. Remember it is human nature to give things to the people
we like and to withhold things from those we dislike. You should
manage this to your advantage.

Almost all cultures feel more sympathetic towards someone who
is smiling. Make sure that you are never accused of having a hard
face. In a tough negotiation you need all the help you can get.

■ Make sure that you have a good solid handshake. A bone crusher
is not the answer, nor a sloppy one.

■ It is almost impossible for human interaction to take place without
good eye contact. You cannot negotiate with sunglasses! Offer
positive eye contact at all times.

■ If you know the name of the people with whom you are
negotiating then you should use these names whenever you are
greeting them. It is human experience from a very early age to
react positively to one's name. You must ensure that you always
spell people's names correctly and pronounce them properly,
especially if you are dealing with people with names from a
different language. Your name is the most powerful word in your
language. Make sure that you understand this. A simple exchange
of business cards will always help you in this respect.

■ Be careful when dealing with people from different cultures so
that you can be sensitive to the difference of behaviour. Do your
homework.

The First Few Steps

■ The best outcome of a negotiation results when you can persuade
the other party to move to your position without having to move
yourself.

- Concentrate on your 'strengths' and not 'weaknesses' ... their 'weaknesses' and not their 'strengths'.

- You must ensure that you retain credibility at all times.

- Your opening should be stretching without being incredible.

- If you aim too low the other party will believe that you will be an easy victim.

- If you aim too high then they may believe that you are not serious.

- Try to reduce the ambitions of the other side and give your arguments more weight.

- If the other party believes that you are not the decision maker then they will either choose not to negotiate or will give you only a small proportion of what is on offer.

- Do not rush. Even if the time-frame is short do not give the impression that you are in a hurry.

- Firstly, if you rush the other side they may perceive that there is too much risk and may walk away.

- Secondly, they may think that you are desperate.

- 'Desperate people agree to desperate deals.'

Testing Questions

- An important skill in negotiation is the ability to ask the right question at the right time.

- In the testing phase of a negotiation meeting ask 'open' questions to find out information and to test.

- An 'open' question begins with the following words: who, what, where, when, how or why.

- An 'open' question forces the other party to reply with information.

- It is very difficult to evade an 'open' question and therefore its use puts the asker in a position of control.

- You should be careful when asking 'why' questions. These can be considered to be abrupt and even threatening: if they explain 'why' and do it, well then, what next?

- Many people mistakenly believe that it is talking that gives you control in a negotiation or sale. This is not the case.

- If you talk too much and are underprepared the other party will put you on the spot with a well-chosen question.

- If you are properly prepared at the beginning of a negotiation you will know what information you require and what assumptions you have made concerning you, your business and the other party.

- Proper use of questions allows you to check out all of this preparation before you move into the next phase of the negotiation when movement starts.

The 'Questioning Path'

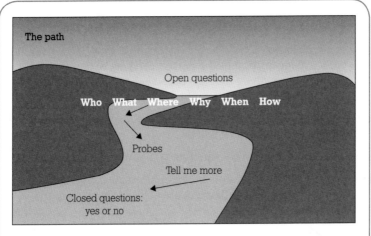

Figure 15.1   The questioning path

- Questioning is a process that is very structured and formalized.

- To obtain the best effect a certain order and style has to be followed, which is best described as the 'questioning path'.

- Going down the questioning path, there are three stages. First are 'open' questions, followed by 'probes', followed lastly by 'closed' questions.

- 'Open' questions elicit information, 'probes' dig deeper and 'closed' questions obtain commitment with a 'yes' or 'no' reply.

■ A 'probe' is an expression such as 'Tell me more about that' or 'I'd like some more information on that particular topic.'
A 'probe' can be framed as either a question or a statement.

■ At the 'close' you can use summary or a restatement.
A good summary gives you control of the meeting and allows you to check that what you heard was in fact correct.
Restatement begins with, 'So what you're saying is …' It allows you to repeat back what you think you heard to check that you are not mistaken.

■ A summary can also be used to move things forward: 'We have covered x, y and z but we need to deal with i, m and n to reach a conclusion.'

Active Listening

■ Active listening is a skill that can be learnt and practised.

■ It is not a passive activity based on 'hearing' what people say, but a proactive means by which a person can ensure that they have understood everything that has been said and at the same time encouraged the speaker to continue.

■ Knowledge is power and in a negotiation the more people tell you the more advantageous it will be.

■ Your first task is to make sure that you always maintain interest.

■ Give good eye contact, nod and offer affirmative noises regularly. This shows the speaker that you are actively engaging in the conversation.

■ Make sure that you do not let your mind wander. Keep focused on what is being said, every single word.

■ You must question the speaker regularly. It shows that you are paying attention and at the same time ensures nothing is said that you may misunderstand.

■ Always try to evaluate any other messages that are coming across, besides the words and their meanings.

■ Does the speaker seem agitated? Is there a tone of voice that is significant?

■ Are there any gestures or body language messages being added to the words that are important?

- Make sure that your own feelings are under control.

- It may be that the other person is not the finest or most interesting speaker, but even if you are bored you must not show it.

- Lastly, suspend your judgement until the end.

- It may be that first impressions were misleading, so give the other person a full chance to make their point before you praise or condemn them.

One-Way Movement

- A key principle of successful negotiation is to seek means by which you can persuade the other party to move from their current position to a new position that is more advantageous to you.

- Many people believe that in order to achieve this movement it is necessary to move oneself by way of offering or trading concessions.

- This may indeed be eventually necessary, but before you even contemplate having to make concessions yourself you should ensure that you have exhausted all the means by which you can persuade the other party to move unilaterally.

- One-way movement is free!

It costs you nothing to employ the best negotiating techniques and may reap major harvests in return.

- **The first and most powerful means by which you can persuade the other party to move is by use of emotion.**
  Emotion seeks to play on the other party's feelings to such an extent that they will willingly move on their own.

- **The second means of persuading people to move unilaterally is by the use of logical reasoning.**
  This seeks to provide evidence, statistics and argument which will ensure that the other party is readily persuaded to move their position. The key word here is 'fact'.

- **The third means is by the use of veiled threat.**
  This seeks to persuade the other party that there is a significant negative consequence attached to their not moving, as a result of which they will happily move towards you.

The Powerful Use of Emotion

- Emotion should always be the first 'out of the box'.

- It is the most powerful means of providing long-term leverage in negotiation.

- The use of warm and friendly appropriate emotion in a negotiation ensures that you and the other party maintain a warm and positive relationship throughout its duration.

- It is an obvious tenet of human nature that we would give things to those who we like and we may even remove things from those we dislike.

- A large number of important decisions are made on emotional grounds.

- Some decisions 'feel' right.

- Advertisers understand the use of emotion very well. Most adverts on the television are based on some form of emotional attachment. Some products and services are sold entirely on emotion. The facts and details take a very firm second place.

- You should always be aware of the cultural nature of emotion.

- It is well known that the British do not show as much emotion as those from southern Europe. This does not mean that emotion is not important for them, but it may be displayed in a different manner. Be aware of this in a negotiation across international cultural boundaries.

Using Logic

- Logical reasoning is often the first and most often used of the negotiator's tools when they are asked to prove a point or justify a position.

- Negotiators who major in this style often carry a laptop computer and have books of facts to prove that they are always correct!

- Logical reasoning is for many people in a negotiation the only means by which they seek to gain advantage. For this reason it is often overused and the other party in the negotiation is usually prepared for it with their own arguments and facts.

- You cannot construct a case without facts and figures, but left to themselves they are vulnerable to a reply based on emotion.

- In reply to a product specification an answer may be, 'I don't like it', or in reply to a price the riposte is 'but I can't afford it.'

- A rule in the use of logical reasoning is that in any battle between numbers it is the first set that grabs the advantage.

- Always tell the other party 'why' before they can tell you 'why not'. That way you always take the initiative and the other party has to respond to your views rather than developing their own argument.

- If you have one really good argument do not dilute it. Many people dilute the strength of their case by adding more unnecessary points.

- Keep to one powerful argument and repeat it if necessary.

- In conversation be careful not to ask the other party why they have reached a certain position. You will be giving them an opportunity to speak in support of their argument. If they have done their preparation they will need no second invitation to put forward their points.

Threat and Coercion

- The use of threat is the third of the one-way movers.

- It is a useful means of persuading the other party to move without having to concede anything in return.

- Threat and coercion are perfectly legitimate tactics in a negotiation when they are practised in a professional and moral manner.

- There can be nothing wrong with the communication to the other party that should they behave in a certain way negative consequences will ensue.

- Threat should be used in small doses and always in a form that is discreet or veiled.

- **Explicit** use of threat causes antagonism and can be counter-productive.

- Using phrases like, 'It would be a shame if I had to look elsewhere' or 'I hope you are not going to force me to have to reduce my order' concentrates the mind of the other party without causing hostility.

- Try to avoid threat against people directly – threaten the organization.

- It is deals, agreements and relationships that are jeopardized by threat, not the individual person. This way, skilful use of threat is rarely seen as a personal hostile act.

- Be very careful about threatening to do something that you are not prepared to carry out – bluff. If your threat is challenged and you subsequently withdraw then your credibility is seriously and maybe even terminally damaged.

Bargaining

- Bargaining occurs in a negotiation when variables start to be exchanged.

- Unlike one-way movement, bargaining means that you must put something on the table to offer in return for something from the other side.

- All the variables in a negotiation must be arranged and valued with a five-stage range for each. You must also try to value the variable from the other party's perspective so that you can gain a true understanding of the value of every element of the deal.

- The true skill of bargaining is to exchange something that has insignificant value for you in return for something that is much more cherished. This is the basis of a sound deal.

- The language of bargaining should be learnt by every negotiator because it is something you will use in many negotiations in which you participate.

- The simplest script is 'If you give me one of yours, then I will give you one of mine.' You can change the words to suit the variables but the principle remains the same.

- You should ensure that you do not expose your position too quickly. A negotiator who has moved once is much more likely to move again.

- Your first move (or attempt to bargain) must be most carefully planned, otherwise you will be educating the other party to become greedy and their expectations will rise.

- Smaller incremental movements act as a disincentive to the other party to keep asking for more.

Read Between the Lines

■ Experienced negotiators always weigh the meaning and tone of their words carefully.

You should not only listen carefully but also try to read the signals that are being transmitted.

■ Congruence is a word which describes the fit between what people say, their tone of voice and their non-verbal signals (body language).

Look at all three before making up your mind that you have understood what they really meant.

What did they mean?	Perhaps they meant ...
It's almost impossible	We can do that – no problem
It's not our regular policy	We can give you a special deal
We don't normally do that	But for you ...
5% is out of the question	How about 4%?
We never admit liability	We can give ex gratia payments
As things stand ...	We're flexible
We'd find that very difficult	It's easy
You must be joking!	You've got a good point
We live in difficult times	Business is good

Thank and Bank

■ Money is not always the subject of a negotiation but in the world of commerce the cost of a deal is paramount.

■ Too many negotiators refuse concessions that are made to them because they are not what they wanted. Never do this.

When you are offered anything in a negotiation there is only one thing to say and that is 'thank you'; and then move to the area or aspect you wanted.

Even if it is not as much as you wanted or if it is not exactly what you require you can say 'thank you' and then bank it.

You can always go for more later. If you reject what is offered then that offer can be withdrawn and then you are even worse off.

■ It is human nature that if we offer something that is then refused, then we are less likely to offer something again in the future.

Here are some scripts that will help:

'Thank you for that. It's a step in the right direction.'

'Thank you for the 5 per cent. It's certainly a help in achieving what I am looking for.'

'That's a good move, thank you; it certainly helps me get closer towards my target.'

'Thank you for that. I think that we'll be quite close to what I want with just a couple more steps.'

And Finally, Remember Tomorrow

■ Experienced negotiators know that they have to take advantage of the immediate opportunity which they are facing.

■ In many organizations you don't get to the long run unless you do well in the short term.

■ It is also paramount that negotiators do not become so focused on the short term that they forget the long-term implications of what they are doing.

■ It is only in a small percentage of negotiations that you will not meet the other party again.

■ It is the essence of good business that you receive repeat orders and nurture long-standing customers and suppliers.

■ Whenever you meet a supplier or customer across the table you can be assured that they will be bringing to the meeting all of the memories of previous negotiations. This baggage can prove very harmful if it is negative.

■ You must see every negotiation as a building block towards a long-term business relationship.

'Know the Rules'

Emotion

■ Use emotion from sincerely held beliefs.

■ Use emotion early.

■ Emotion can counter logic.

- Use emotion to increase the perceived value of your bargaining (straw issue).

Logical Reasoning
- Do not be quick to ask 'Why?' You may get a number of very good reasons which could make refusal difficult.

- Get your logic in first.

- Do not dilute your argument with too much logic. Remember KISS (Keep It Simple Stupid).

- Do not waste your logic on someone who will never see it. Change your persuasion behaviour.

Threat
- Do not be too quick to use threat.

- Hint at threat. Use mirrored or remote threat.

- Threat at business level, not personal level.

- Never make a threat you cannot carry out.

- Add threat to bargaining by adding 'if'.

Bargaining
- Do not expose your position (at least not too quickly).

- Do not be too eager to show you are prepared to move.

- When you do move, do so in small steps.

- Thank – for any concession given, this takes ownership.

- Give things that are cheap for things of value.

Compromise
- Compromise is a behaviour of last resort.

- Do not be too quick to compromise.

- 50:50 is not the only compromise.

- Compromise favours the person who takes the more extreme position.

- The party who suggests a compromise will probably accept the other position.

Consider your Variables

Contractual	**Pricing**
Buy back	Volume discounts
Consequential aspects	Rebates
Duration	Breakdown/analysis
Liquidated damages	Stability
Terms and conditions	Deferral of increase
Third party liability	Payment terms
Authorship of contract	Currency
Health and safety	Installation costs
Insurance	Delivery costs
Inventory	**Relationship**
Buffer stocks	Confidentiality
Consignment stocks	Exclusivity
Collection of surplus	Sole supplier
Spares	Risk sharing
Unit of issue	Flexibility to changes
	'Guinea pig' to customer
Product	Supply chain
Assistance with trials	Audit rights
Commissioning	
Customization	**Specification**
Free samples	Manuals/drawings
Developments	Plans/critical path
Product endorsement	Training
	Performance guarantees
Production	Materials for testing
Quality/reliability	Tool kits
Supply security	Packaging
Flexibility	Progress reports
Lead time	Emergency response
Just in time	Translations

Appendices

A Strategic Context for Negotiation and Commercial Relationships

1

In this appendix I show further use of supply positioning and supplier preferencing by comparing the position of the two in a buying and selling scenario and how it may impact on any negotiation.

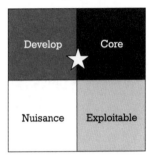

Example 1: Top box negotiations and relationships are based on a strong need to work together over the potential long term. Both parties have a vested interest in maintaining good business and personal relations.

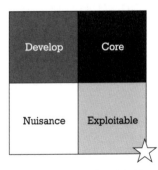

Example 2: Negotiations and relationships with tactical profit and exploitable elements are based on the need to compete and play against rather than with the other party. These are not pretty and will be adversarial and at arm's length.

Buyer's Perspective

Seller's Perspective

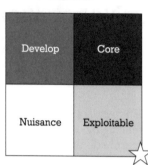

Example 3: Negotiations and relationships which are drawn from the top and bottom of the four box models are a clear imbalance where one party seeks to look at the future prospects while the other is seeking only a short-term advantage. The Strategic side of the negotiation is very vulnerable.

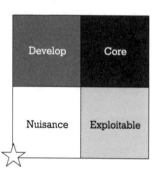

Example 4: Any combination with a Tactical Acquisition or Nuisance ingredient is likely to be at arm's length and may be based on only a flimsy need to do business. It is not the likely basis of any long-term arrangement that is detailed and complex.

2

Strategic Relationship Building

Relationship questions	Outcome questions
Is there a relationship?	Do you need to win at all costs?
Is it positive or negative?	How many points can you concede?
Is a future relationship desirable?	Is your reputation on the line?
What is the length and history?	What is the power balance?
What is the level of commitment?	Have you surveyed your strengths and weaknesses AND THEIRS?
What is the level of co-dependence?	Are there issues of principle here?
How much open communication exists?	Who won last time?

Hi

This is a business deal where the quality of the relationship takes absolute precedence. It may be a monopoly situation where alternative strategies are not available or it could be a political problem where a short-term business sacrifice is worth it in the long run. It may be that considerations outside the parameters of the deal need to be taken into account

Accommodating Negotiations	**Collaborative Negotiations**
Lose to win relationships	**Win/Win Relationships**
Given value Passive threat	**Created Value Goodwill Trust**
0 + 4 = 4 (It's the long view)	**2 + 2 = 5** (Let's work together)

This is both a relationship and a business need of the highest order. Working together will create value and allow opportunities to be realized. At some stage the value will need to be allocated but in early stages of the deal it is a relationship-based activity with the long view in mind. The people skills of the occupants will be at a premium in order to release potential synergy

These negotiations take place with a firm hand on the terms and conditions. Negotiators are concerned to do what is right and proper according to obligations. The relationship will often be at arm's length and governed by business rather than feelings

Importance of the Relationship

Transactional Negotiations	**Persuasive Negotiations**
Cautious Relationships	**Win/Perceived Win Relationships**
Agreed Value Contractual Trust	**Negotiated Value Incremental Trust**

This is a lively negotiation where the interests of one side are protected but not at the expense of the long-term relationship. These negotiators wish to win and win again and need to leave the other party just happy enough to wish to continue

There are times when neither the business nor the relationship justifies any activity and opportunities are just not worth pursuing. It may be that the business is reaching a natural conclusion and that this is a symptom of its end

Avoiding Negotiations	**Opportunistic Negotiations**
Lose/Lose Relationships	**Win/Lose Relationships**
Commodity Value Competence Trust	**Claimed Value No Trust**
? + ? = ? (Who cares?)	**3 + 1 = 4** (I'll fight you)

This is a zero sum game negotiation and the result is more important than the quality of any ensuing relationship. It is a highly adversarial Tactical Profit environment and not one where sensitive managers will want to be for any length of time. Your objective is to seize value from the other side. It is a fight over crumbs, not an effort to grow the cake. There are usually only short-term objectives to be achieved

Lo ←———— *Importance of the Outcome* ————→ Hi

3

The 25 Steps to Testing Your Own Negotiation Skills

Everyone can benefit from this 'health check' devised by the Negotiation Resource International arm of PMMS Consulting Group.[3]

Negotiation involves a complete complement of interpersonal, selling and negotiation skills in order to breed success time after time in the business environment in which you work.

Test your strengths and style with this quick but revealing questionnaire. When you finish, check the analysis to see where there is room for improvement.

To start, circle the answers that best apply to you.

Your options are:

1: Never
2: Occasionally
3: Frequently
4: Always

1.	I research the other party before I enter into negotiations	1	2	3	4
2.	I choose negotiation tactics that are appropriate to my objectives	1	2	3	4
3.	I read background material before I devise my strategy	1	2	3	4
4.	I consciously use body language to communicate with the other party	1	2	3	4
5.	I communicate my points logically and clearly	1	2	3	4

---

3 Adapted from an NRI Exercise created by R.L. Sandford.

6.	I regularly summarize the progress that has been made during negotiations	1	2	3	4
7.	I work well as a member of a negotiation team	1	2	3	4
8.	I know who my internal customers are and understand their business needs	1	2	3	4
9.	I have clear measures of success for each of my objectives	1	2	3	4
10.	I assess the risk in every decision I make	1	2	3	4
11.	I listen very carefully to my customers' needs	1	2	3	4
12.	I communicate the right message to the right person at the right time	1	2	3	4
13.	I project self-confidence and speak confidently	1	2	3	4
14.	I try to exclude personal prejudices of all kinds when judging others	1	2	3	4
15.	I know my own strengths at work and use them to the fullest	1	2	3	4
16.	I listen carefully to opposing views before summarizing them	1	2	3	4
17.	I keep up to date with developments within my industry	1	2	3	4
18.	I am proactive and am always looking for new opportunities	1	2	3	4
19.	I use my voice and hands to emphasize suggestions	1	2	3	4
20.	I am specific about asking for what I want and for what I need	1	2	3	4

21.	I regularly mix with new people and build new contacts	1	2	3	4
22.	I make a point of learning new sales skills and techniques	1	2	3	4
23.	I identify the customers' needs and change my approach accordingly	1	2	3	4
24.	I endeavour to get the other party to name their objectives first	1	2	3	4
25.	I get feedback to ensure that my customers are very satisfied with the purchase/sale	1	2	3	4

As this exercise demonstrates, negotiation involves looking at the effectiveness of your own personal behaviour, your influencing skills, your communication style, your understanding of the seller/buyer and recognizing and using negotiation strategies and tactics that work in your particular environment.

The answers you gave will add up to a total points score. Now you can check it against the following analysis – encouraging you to look at your current skill set and recognize where you might develop your skills further.

25–60

Your negotiation skills are weak. Are you putting the customers first or are you doing what you have always done? You may consider how well you are communicating with colleagues and internal customers. You may consider how well you understand your influencing skills and think about a new approach to the behaviour you are currently demonstrating in relationships. You may need to understand selling skills in more detail – you may be in a role that is demanding higher selling skills and this may be affecting your current performance.

60–85

You have reasonable negotiation skills, but certain areas need further improvement. Are you receiving enough practical experience in the workplace at high-level negotiations? You are aware that your customers are important to you, but your communication skills may be letting you down so that people are misinterpreting your key messages when you thought that all issues were clearly communicated. You probably recognize that business relationships are important to you but perhaps find that you don't always make this a priority in the workplace. You are aware that good negotiators are good sellers but may benefit from further information about what makes an effective seller.

85+

Your recognition of selling, communication, influencing, behavioural and negotiation skills is high. However, I would always recommend that you continue to work on improving your abilities in order to stay at the top and continually keep that business edge. Learning never stops for you. You are a proactive and keen individual who recognizes opportunities for growth and development. You are a skilled influencer who relates easily with others and probably finds communication skills easy.

You probably do put the customer first and avoid complacency in the workplace by continually requesting feedback. Your negotiations are more frequently successful than not, but the fact that you are continually striving for improvement means that you want to know skills that will help you to retain your strength in negotiation. For that reason, I recommend that you review your selling, influencing, behavioural and communication skills on a regular basis.

4

The Florida Story

The Scenario

Imagine you are taking a well-earned holiday on a beautiful island off the Florida coast. Walking along the beach one evening with your partner and three teenage children you bump into a major client – also with their partner and three children. Once the surprise of this unexpected encounter passes you invite the client together with family to celebrate Easter Sunday with you at a brunch for all ten of you. The venue is the restaurant, overlooking the Caribbean, in the complex you are staying at.

You agree to meet at 12.30 pm in the bar next to the restaurant for a champagne brunch at 1 pm (cost $75 per head). You meet in the bar and once everyone is seated and has a drink you check in with the restaurant manager, who states that he will come and get you as soon as your table is ready. At 1.30 pm, ordering a second round of drinks you decide to prompt the restaurant manager regarding being asked to go to your table. The restaurant manager apologizes for keeping you waiting, states that they have been extremely busy and he will come and get you in a few moments.

He actually doesn't call you to your table until 2.15 pm and when the waiter comes to take your order you find that some of your favourites on the menu are no longer available. However, there are several bottles of champagne on the table and the food is generally good. At around about 3.30 pm the waiter comes along to take your orders for pudding but in doing so states that the blueberry pie and all other options are sold out and that all he can offer you is to personally make you a hot fudge sundae for each of the ten of you. This he does and they are very good but not what you would have asked for normally.

When the bill is presented you refuse to sign and ask to see the restaurant manager, to whom you simply state: 'I am not prepared to sign this bill at this point in time [$750] and I would like to see you and the general manager in his office to discuss this during the next week of my stay here.'

That evening all ten of you walk down the Caribbean beach and discuss objectives for the forthcoming meeting with the restaurant manager and general manager.

Write down your objective below. Make it clear before referring over the page.

Objective

The Outcome

You and your client decide to go along together to meet the two men. It was decided that during your opening you would focus on emotion and not put a *marker* down thus giving your objective away. You took ten minutes or thereabouts explaining what happened and detailing how it left you feeling and upsetting the day. At the end of this introduction it was agreed you would both go silent. After approximately 20 seconds, which seemed like two minutes, the general manager turned to his restaurant manager and said the following: 'I am highly embarrassed by what has happened here and I can't apologize enough to these people. There is no question of you paying any part of this bill, gentlemen. You must also to assuage my uncomfortableness here join me with your families at a complimentary dinner during this coming week.'

Analysis

Refer back to the objective you wrote after the scenario on the previous page. Ask yourself: 'Did that objective and potential opening you used limit the outcome that I would obtain?' Simply put, would it allow me to get a position where I did not pay for brunch and get another free meal as well?

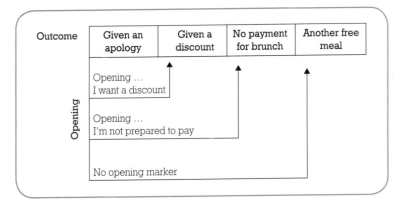

Outcome	Given an apology	Given a discount	No payment for brunch	Another free meal
Opening … I want a discount				
Opening … I'm not prepared to pay				
No opening marker				

The more you aim for the more you get, but do not reveal your aim during the opening phase and preferably not at any time if possible.

Further Reading

Back K and Back K, *Assertiveness at Work: A Practical Guide to Handling Awkward Situations*, McGraw Hill, 2005.

Beckett I, *The First World War: The Essential Guide to Sources in the UK National Archives*, Richmond, 2002, p.27.

Brown JM, Berrien FK and Russell DL, *Applied Psychology*, Macmillan, 1966.

Cox A, The Power Perspective in Procurement and Supply Management, *Journal of Supply Chain Management*, March 2001.

CRC, Yoshimori M, *Doing Business in Japan*, SRI International.

CRC Negotiations Seminar, Mezouar M, *Doing Business on the Arabian Peninsula*, SRI International.

Fayerweather J and Kapoor A, *Strategy and Negotiation for the International Corporation: Guidelines and Cases*, Ballinger, 1976.

Fisher R and Ury W, *Getting to Yes: Negotiating Agreement Without Giving In*, Houghton Mifflin, 1981.

Hofstede G, *Culture's Consequences: Comparing Values, Behaviours, Institutions and Organisations Across Nations*, Sage, 2001.

Karass CL, *Give and Take: The Complete Guide to Negotiating Strategies and Tactics*, HarperBusiness, 1993.

Kennedy G, *Pocket Negotiator*, Profile in association with the Economist Newspaper, 1997.

Kraus D, Terpend R and Peterson KJ, Bargaining Stances and Outcomes in Buyer–Seller Negotiations: Experimental Results, *Journal of Supply Chain Management*, Volume 43, Issue 3, July 2006.

McCracken GK and Callahan TJ, Is there such a thing as a free lunch?, *International Journal of Purchasing and Materials Management*, December 1996.

Mehrabian A, *Silent Messages: Implicit Communication of Emotions and Attitudes*, Wadsworth, 1981.

Nierenberg G, *Fundamentals of Negotiating*, Hawthorne Books, 1973.

Pease A, *Body Language: How to Read Others' Thoughts by Their Gestures*, Sheldon Press, 1997.

Pilling BK and Zhang L, Cooperative Exchange: Rewards and Risks, *International Journal of Purchasing and Materials Management*, March 1992.

Rackham N and Carlisle J, The Effective Negotiator – Part 2: Planning for Negotiations, *Journal of European Industrial Training*, Volume 2, Number 7, 1978.

Rognes J, Negotiating Cooperative Relationships: A Planning Framework, *International Journal of Purchasing Materials Management*, September 1995.

Sako M, Buyers, Suppliers and Trust in Japanese Business, *Journal of International Logistics*, June 1992.

Steele PT and Beasor T, *Business Negotiation: A Practical Workbook*, Gower, 1999.

Steele PT and Court BH, *Profitable Purchasing Strategies: A Manager's Guide for Improving Organisational Competitiveness Through the Skills of Purchasing*, McGraw Hill, 1996.

Trompenaars A and Hampden-Turner C, *Riding the Waves of Culture: Understanding Cultural Diversity in Business*, Nicholas Brealey, 1997.

Index

Index